BAGGY PANTS & WARM BEER

First edition, published in 2007 by

WOODFIELD PUBLISHING
Bognor Regis, West Sussex PO21 5EL
United Kingdom
www.woodfieldpublishing.com

ISBN 1-84683-041-9

Baggy Pants
& Warm Beer

PETER OUTRIDGE

Woodfield

Dedicated to all who served in the
504th PIR during World War Two

Memorial Stone to the men of the 82nd Airborne Division.
Victoria Park, Leicester.

Dedicated by General Matthew Ridgeway on 11th May 1976. The inscription reads:

**IN TRIBUTE AND
MEMORY OF THOSE MEN OF
THE UNITED STATES (ALL AMERICAN)
82ND AIRBORNE DIVISION
WHO SERVED IN LEICESTER AND COUNTY
PRIOR TO THE "D" DAY INVASION OF
EUROPE 1944**

**They came in freedom, They fought with gallantry
Many never to return to their Homeland.**

"Devils in Baggy Pants".

From an entry found in the diary of a German officer killed at Anzio:

"American parachutists -- devils in baggy pants -- are less than 100 meters from my outpost line. I can't sleep at night; they pop up from nowhere and we never know when or how they will strike next. Seems like the black-hearted devils are everywhere..."

An early 504 Parachute Infantry Regimental Pocket Patch.

An excerpt from a report on an early fact finding visit to England by Captain Beall of HQ Company, 1st Battalion 504 printed in the regiment's newspaper "Prop-Blast" dated October 1942 (perhaps a taste of things to come for the men of the 504) Capt. Beall was later killed in action in Sicily whilst Executive Officer for 3rd Battalion:

"British people generally are swell, but are so rationed they can give little to American troops, but they offer it all, without question. Girls appreciate stockings and lipstick most for gifts.

The low pay of British soldiers occasionally causes bad feeling. Their parachutists, with jump pay, get only $15 a month. The beer there now is very flat and weak, whisky very hard to get."

Front Cover Picture: Left to right, 1st Sgt. A. Tarbell H Company, Sgt.J.P. Brettand H Company, Unknown paratrooper - probably also H Company.

Contents.

A Paratroopers Prayer.

God All Mighty!
In a few short hours we will be in battle with the enemy.
We do not join battle afraid.
We do not ask favours or indulgence
But ask that if You will use us as Your instruments
For the right and an aid in returning peace to the world.
We do not know or seek what our fate will be
We ask only this,
That if die we must, that we die as men would die,
Without pleading and safe in the feeling
That we have done our best
For what we believed was right.
Oh Lord! Protect our loved ones.
Be near us in the fire ahead and
With us now as we pray to You,

Amen

Forword

By Walter E. Hughes
I Company, 3rd Battalion, 504th Parachute Infantry Regiment.

Through the modern magic, or rather the technology of the computer and the wonderment of E-Mail, the author Peter Outridge and I have become as close as if we were living next door to one another. In this book we are sharing a segment of our lives that was also part of a devastating war. Peter grew up in a town that I as a soldier in the 82nd Airborne Division was fortunate enough to spend a very short and peaceful time in during WW II. For a combat soldier in a Parachute Unit such as my regiment, the 504th PIR, there were only brief periods where your unit was resting or re-organizing, even then the training continued. This book by Peter Outridge is about soldiers and the people of the town of Leicester and the area around it. It is about war, for if it were not for the war, it would not have been written. But it is about the good side of a war, if you can call anything about a war good.

The 504 was part of the 82nd Airborne Division, but when the Division was moved from Italy to the UK in 1944, after the Battle of Anzio, General Mark Clark requested that the 504 remain with the 5th Army in Italy. His request was honored and the 82nd sailed for England to prepare for the assault on Normandy. The 508 PIR recently arrived in England replaced the 504, which had continued to fight the enemy in Italy.

When finally relieved by General Clark the Regiment rejoining the Division in England, because of the heavy casualties it was sorely in need of replacements and most of all for the tired GI's, rest. Enter the citizens of Leicester. Warmly greeted by the people, the soldiers were like sponges; they absorbed the kindness, the hospitality and the friendship of the people. They spoke the same language (well almost), the pubs were not unlike our own back in the States, and for a few short months from April to September 1944 a bond between soldiers far from home and civilians suddenly exposed to the (at times) strange Americans, were cemented. It was a good period, I was a part of that time, it was a time I will never forget, and it was a time that helped me to survive the ordeals of that war. Perhaps by the memories this book has brought back, I can still be a part of that time again.

I wish to thank Peter Outridge for letting me be a small part of his book and to the people I was so lucky to know from that time, many I never even knew their names,

Thank You.

Walter E. Hughes

Introduction

I first became interested in the US Army's 504 Parachute Infantry Regiment (PIR) 82nd Airborne Division when my partners brother-in-law, a former US Marine and 1st Gulf War veteran who is very interested in military history, invited me to get involved in a living history re-enactment of a small part of the 82nd and 101st Airborne Divisions drop into Normandy on the night of the 5th/6th of June 1944. It seemed like a good idea at the time, I have served with the Royal Air Force, and the Territorial Army; (6(v) Battalion, Royal Anglian Regiment), so have something of a military background. I'd been interested in World War 2 and the 1940's for some time, having been to a number of D-Day 60th Anniversary commemorative events during the summer of 2004. We were also by complete coincidence going to be on holiday in the region at a time that this particular event had been planned - it was organised by the owner of the French Gite (holiday cottage) that we were to stay at.

"A Devil in Baggy Pants" - Every inch a Paratrooper and obviously very proud of it!

I decided right up front that a little digging for information was called for (the "little digging" soon became quite a large excavation as these things sometimes have a habit of doing, hence the book you are reading now!), just so I would have some idea of the background to the operation and the units involved. It didn't take me long to discover that units of the 82nd Airborne Division had been billeted all over my home county of Leicestershire during the period, and that the 504 PIR in particular had actually been billeted at Shady Lane, Evington, (although it would appear - up until now - little has been written about this period of their WW2 history). This was only about a mile from where I was born and spent my childhood and early teenage years.

I lived in Oadby, a village just south of Evington in Leicestershire, and used to spend many happy and exciting hours during the long school summer holidays playing adventurous games of war in and around what we imaginatively knew as "Ghost Town". In reality these old derelict Nissen huts and buildings had once been part of RAF Leicester East Airfield at nearby Stoughton. (My father had been an Air Cadet with the local Air Training Corps' 1461 Squadron during the war, and remembers vividly hanging around the airfield in their uniforms scrounging joy rides from the "Yanks" in the C47 Dakota's that operated out of there at the time. The airfield still exists today and is home to the Leicester Aero Club - where my father learned to fly back in the 1960's - and a Go-karting club amongst other organisations).

It was only natural then, that I should represent a trooper from the 504 during the re-enactment in Normandy. The only problem was, as my investigations soon found out, the 504 (as a unit) didn't take part in the D-Day operation, however small numbers were involved as security details attached to the pathfinders for the 507 and 508 PIR, so pathfinder security I would have to be.

This book is not essentially a military history; there are lots of excellent publications that do justice to the 504 PIR's fine combat record during the Second World War, what I have attempted to do is to tell the story of a five month period in 1944 when the men of the 504 PIR, battered and bruised from campaigns in North Africa, Sicily, and Italy, found themselves neighbours and in a lot of cases good friends to the villagers of Evington, Stoughton and Oadby in Leicestershire, England, and is dedicated to all those who served with the 504 Parachute Infantry Regiment during World War Two.

I would also like to dedicate this, with my grateful thanks to all those individuals (notably Walter E. Hughes, and Deryk Wills) from both sides of the Atlantic (and elsewhere – notably Frank van Lunteren from Holland) who have contributed their help and memories, and the time to relate them to me, as without them, I'd never have got the project finished!

(As a footnote; if you are a 504 veteran of WW2, or relative of a 504 veteran, or a local Leicester person and upon reading this book you feel you could contribute memories of the time the 504 PIR spent in Leicestershire during 1944 I would be very glad to hear from you. If sufficient new material comes to light, then I would be prepared to produce a second updated edition. My contact details can be found at the back of the book).

Chapter 1.

Better Times Just Around the Corner.
(Anzio: Italy to Evington: England).

The 504's time in Italy had been unquestionably tough although enemy losses had exceeded those of the regiment by ten to one. They were pulled out of the line at the Anzio beachhead and boarded landing craft on 23rd March 1944 to returned to Naples, and shortly afterwards, on the 11th April boarded the British troopship "Capetown Castle" and sailed for England escorted by sleek British and Canadian destroyers. However, not all the 'troopers were that keen to leave Italy, Bill Leonard (right) of I Company recalls one George Leolis, also affectionately known as 'the Greek', 'the Crusso', or 'the Lover' (he was obviously a real character!); *"We had to tie him up to get him aboard ship for England. He wanted to fight and retake Naples again – from the MP's!"*

 Lt. Roy Hanna (left) of G Company on the other hand was so keen to leave that he begged the regiments Commanding Officer Colonel Tucker from his sick bed in a Naples hospital not to be left behind (he had been seriously wounded in the chest whilst at Anzio in an action for which he won the DSC), and so spent the voyage and most of his time in England recovering and playing cards (mostly Bridge he recalls) with the Battalion Medical Staff.

Two of Hitler's radio propaganda personalities (Axis?) Sally and George, who had become acquainted with the 504 during their time in Italy (and who seemed remarkably well informed), told men of the regiment in a farewell transmission that they would never make British waters, and would indeed be sunk by U boats before they sailed through the Straits of Gibraltar. However, the only danger the ship encountered on the voyage was self inflicted, and came when all the troops rushed to the same side of the vessel to get an eyeful of a ferryboat load of energetically waving girl's that

The Capetown Castle

steamed past the ship as it pulled into port. The ship (all 27,000 tons of her), listed heavily to port and the Captain was heard to broadcast out of the ships tannoy authoritatively (and one suspects with not a little alarm in his voice) *"Attention, Attention trim ship. Troops must not congregate on one rail. If order is not maintained, it will be necessary to clear the deck."* The ship was trimmed and balance restored, but only after the Regiments Commanding Officer, Colonel Tucker broadcast to his men to "spread", which they immediately did. Aboard the Capetown Castle, not un-naturally there was now a buzz of excitement among the paratroopers… "Did you see the dame in the yellow sweater, Holy cats?"

Sgt. Ross Carter wrote of their voyage in his book "Those Devils in Baggy Pants":

"Aboard were superbly disciplined tall, lean, dry-skinned, powerfully built Scots, Irish, and Coldstream Guards, wearing standard British battle dress which they always kept neat and spotless, making the long voyage home after five or six years' service for the King in the far corners of the world.

By contrast the 'troopers resembled a mob of pirates. Nearly all of us, dressed in anything from fatigues to tan jump suites, wore a handlebar moustache and shuffled around with a pistol or knife or both swinging on our shoulder or hip. I am certain that, in modern times, a more desperate-looking gang of ruffians had not sailed on a British ship.

The British Guardsmen, knowing us to be one of the crack regiments of the American Army, surveyed us with undisguised amazement and curiosity. To them discipline was an important factor in war, and if we had any, they couldn't put their finger on it!"

Darrell G. Harris of Hq & Hq Company remembered the voyage in his memoirs (entitled Casablanca to VE Day):

"The Capetown Castle was better than the George Washington (the troopship that had carried the regiment from America to North Africa in1943) *in some respects, but worse in others. We were quartered in plywood shelters that had been erected on the main deck. We got plenty of fresh air, which was better. Breakfast usually consisted of dried herring and cold oatmeal, which was worse. There was a contingency of Irish Guards on board, and they played a bagpipe concert every afternoon on the forward deck. This was considered good by some and bad by others, depending on each individual's ear for music. I have always found bagpipe music quite stirring, so I enjoyed those concerts, and I believe most of the other guys did too."*

Pvt. Eddie Livingston of I Company recalls that the 504 'troopers ran an "Invasion Lottery" whilst on the voyage back from Italy, and he drew three dates, the 5th 6th and 7th June (at a Dollar a date). Eddie subsequently volunteered for pathfinder duties for the D-Day operations and gave his tickets for safe keeping to his buddy's girlfriend in Leicester, one Olive Weir. Sadly Eddie never got to collect his winnings as he was taken as a prisoner of war on June 9th, never returning to England, and his friend was seriously injured and evacuated back to America. (So if Olive or any of her family is still out there, and you have those tickets, you could be sitting on a small fortune!!)

Pvt. Louis C. Marino of A Company remembered the trip from Naples to England and the time he stayed in Leicester:

"We came back to Naples and got on a boat called the Capetown Castle. It was a big ship; it was a converted English luxury liner I think. It was about the same size as the George Washington that originally took us overseas. The weather was beautiful going through the Mediterranean and it was a really pretty sight going through the Straits of Gibraltar and going to England.

Just outside Leicester we stayed in a town right at the golf course. We had a nice setup there while we were in Leicester until we went to Holland. We had passes to go into town all the time drinking beer".

Pvt. Louis C. Marino of A Company at the regimental camp site, Shady Lane. (Courtesy of Frank van Lunteren).

The 504 arrived at Liverpool on 22nd April 1944, the paratroopers were strangely thoughtful; they may have been quietly excited perhaps because they were looking for the first time at English soil, and from where they stood it looked pretty

A very busy Liverpool Docks during 1944 – The 504 arrived here on 22 April

good (and so did the girls!) – Certainly not as they had expected. The British Guardsmen, who had returned with the 504, (some of which had also fought on the Anzio beach-head), appeared thoughtful as well. They were seeing England not for the first time in their lives, but for the first time in several years and they too, seemed to be contrasting the peace and tranquillity of the riverbank with the wreckage and death that had been war torn Italy.

Lt. Carl Mauro recalls *"the wharves of Liverpool, where we docked, were a beautiful sight to the battle weary veterans. The red rooftops of the Liverpudlian homes and buildings shone brightly in the spring sunshine. We entered another world, different from Naples, Anzio, Sicily, and North Africa. We entered a domain more like America."*

That night at 11 o'clock the troops staggered down the gangplank carrying two barracks bags and full field equipment, they fell in on the pier and marched through Liverpool's blacked out streets to the railway station. They then endured an all night train ride south to Leicestershire and at about 10 o'clock the next morning the train pulled into a little country station, Thurnby & Scraptoft where they were greeted by the 82nd Airborne Division band playing "The All American Soldier". Generals Ridgeway and Gavin were also amongst many others there to greet the Regiment back into the fold. Pfc. Paul H. Pannell, HQ Company. 2nd Battalion, from Arizona, who was a mortar man recalls that there was a white

Thurnby & Scraptoft Railway Station

picket fence around the station, with a swing gate off the platform to the road, he vividly remembers General Ridgeway standing at that gate saluting each and every 'trooper as they passed through as a mark of respect and gratitude for what they had achieved whilst fighting under General Mark Clark in Italy.

The 82nd Airborne Division Band

The 'troopers then formed up and marched heads held high the last couple of miles to their destination which was the regimental holding area at Shady Lane in Evington, just outside Leicester, and it turned out to be quite pleasant. They were to be billeted in tents as the wooden huts enjoyed by the Italian and German Prisoners of War who came after the 504 left had not yet been built, but the green grass was soft underfoot and there were toilets and mess halls and unlike North Africa and Italy, there was no dust (and nobody shooting at them). There were gravel walks and company streets laid out in neat rows. Everything had been done in advance, and in each tent were five camp beds - strictly a luxury item so far as the men of 504 had been concerned during the past year - and on each camp bed there were two new blankets.

Picture Postcard of Shady Lane, Evington, hard to date, but my guess is this is what it looked like when the 504 were there.

Corporal Fred J. Baldino of A Company who spent his 22nd birthday at Anzio and had been promoted, was one of the troopers who arrived on the Capetown Castle, he remembers:

"After we got to England, after coming up through 9 months of combat in Italy, it was almost like coming home. The people spoke English, they had beer in the pubs and there was plenty, plenty, plenty girls where we were stationed up in the Midlands (Leicester) and we were all catching up on lost time. When we first got to England from Italy, my Squad didn't have any replacements. But as we stayed on there, they eventually replaced all the missing spots in the Regiment and in a month or so we were back at full capacity. In that period between May and September I had re-unions with three different brothers who were in different divisions. One (Leo) had gotten frozen feet at the front and was back in England and he and I got together quite a bit, a lot of times on double dates. "

Lt. R. Breard, A Company XO comments; *"We thought we were in Heaven living in tents, even though on arrival we were detained in camp for more or less the first two weeks. As I recall, every afternoon well-dressed local residents would walk by looking at us as if we were in a zoo!*

Although we were in England to rest, things were not to be that easy, first thing every day we would jog through the neighbourhood loudly counting cadence just as we did back at Ft. Benning, Georgia. I suppose at one time or another we must have woken everyone in Evington, Stoughton, and Oadby".

Terence Cartwright (a local youngster at the time) remembers the Shady Lane camp:

A high altitude picture of the 504's regimental holding area on Shady Lane. The rows of tents can clearly be seen.

"I had the unforgettable experience of tasting my first Wrigley's Spearmint Chewing Gum. Tents had appeared over night, like Magic Mushroom's, and within these miniature Aladdin's Caves, trestle tables groaned under the weight of 'Camel' Cigarettes, chewing gum, tins of exotic meats and foods we had never seen or tasted before. These treasures' were dispensed by 'Gods (who spoke like the 'Dead End Kids' and 'Roy Rogers' combined) to the hoards of grubby, green-candle nosed, ragged trouser-bottomed 'Dennis the Menace' and

'Just William' look-a-likes who descended on the camp like locusts... Yes... The Yanks had arrived!"

Another local lad, Dennis Neal, wrote in his wartime memories:

"I remember well the arrival of the Yanks, as we saw many of them in Hart Road chasing the

pretty girls. Indeed one of the girls, Joan Beard, married one and went away to Washington as a GI bride. I have memories of walking to Evington Lane where airborne troops were in a tent camp and even to Stoughton airfield where I watched huge gliders being towed into the air, released and landing back at the airfield, all part of the build up to D-Day. The skies on those late evenings of double summer time were a mass of aircraft."

The Author at the junction of Gartree Rd. and Shady Lane, Evington, the 504's camp site lay just beyond the hedgerow

Mr. A. R. Pendell, a resident of Oadby at the time recalls:

"I grew up in Oadby, just across the road from where a Vehicle Maintenance Unit, attached to the U.S. 82nd Airborne Division were billeted in Sandhurst Street, and have many memories of playing ball games with G.I.'s in the park next to the billets. Some became friends to the youngsters and their families. One soldier called Max still writes regularly to one of my friends. The American canteen Lorries used to come down our street and sell doughnuts and hotdogs. Every time they came, the cry would go up 'Yankee lorry!' 'Yankee lorry!' and the street would suddenly be filled with scruffy kids racing to buy these goodies."

John Morrison, an inquisitive nine year old back in 1944, recalls walking passed the camp one

Above: Aerial view of the 504's Shady Lane site taken in 1945, it was used as a repatriation centre and PoW camp after the paratroopers left. Worn patches in the grass field (top centre) show where some of their tents had been pitched.

day with a friend and coming across a 504 'trooper sitting cross-legged in the middle of a small square area surrounded by a trench on all four sides. The trench was immaculately dug, with all corners accurately cut, and the grass neatly swept. Being nine years old, and naturally curious, John asked the 'trooper what he was doing, to which he replied, "I've been a bad, bad boy".

I related this story to Jim McIver, a veteran of 504 Service Company that I had the privilege to meet, and he explained: "ah, a six-by-six, the guy was on field punishment, he would

have had to dig the trench out in a square shape, six by six, and usually about 18 inches wide and 2 feet deep, then stay within it's confines until the officer of the day had inspected his handy-work (casually tossed his cigarette butt in) and told him to fill it in".

Derek Chapman, another young lad at the time remembers:

"When I was a boy of about eleven during the war, the Americans stationed units of the 82nd Airborne Division on the Evington (Leicester) golf course. We lads used to go up there in the evening and fetch beer for them from the local off-license. We got to know some of them pretty well. They were warm friendly generous young men in the peak of physical condition. We did this for some months. We used to watch the paratroopers playing cards, money meant nothing to them. There was often a pile of English pound notes 5 or 6 inches high in the middle! I still think of them with great affection and wonder how many of them survived the war."

The Author takes a break at the Shady Lane site, today it is a country park

Francis was about fifteen at the time, and helped his father out at the family-run bicycle shop in Evington. They supplied many bicycles to the visiting Americans, and fixed endless punctures*. In common with a lot of local youngsters during this period, he used to run errands for some of the paratroopers and became quit close to several. One in particular called "Red" (on account of his ginger hair) who used to call on the family, and was often invited for meals.

On one occasion he was walking through the fields between St. Deny's church and the brook at the bottom of Shady Lane with a couple of friends when they strayed inadvertently close to where the paratroopers had a hand-grenade practice range, (which was surrounded by safety nets). Unfortunately at the time a practice session was taking place and the three got completely showered with mud and debris from an exploding 'grenade, luckily for them, other than being shaken up they were unharmed. All three were taken to the camp medical section where they were cleaned up and checked over by the medical staff, who were full of apologies for the incident.

Ivan Rawson, a thirteen-year-old local lad has similar memories of the "Yanks at Stoughton Golf Course" (this was actually the Leicestershire Golf Course):

"As a thirteen year old with mates we used to visit the camp on the Stoughton Golf Course. We took candles and coat hangers to the GI's in exchange for cigarettes, sweets (candy as the Yanks used to call it) and gum. We also used to fetch beer and snacks from the off licence for those who were confined to camp for various reasons such as failing to jump when on training flights around the area. They used to sit by the perimeter playing dice (craps). On the opposite side of the road was an area where they had a full sized boxing ring and training bouts with some very good fighters from the Golden Glove Tournaments in America. They used the silk from their parachutes as robes. We also went to a boxing night at De Montfort Hall where they fought British boxers.

Some of the GI's used to ask us to loan our bikes to go and meet the local girls. Later on when I got a job as pot boy at the Craddock Arms in Knighton (right), there used to be a shortage of beer, and sometimes the pub would be

6

"closed", that was unless you knew the secret knock – which the GI's soon learnt; they were very good customers. They did used to complain about the warm beer though. They used to leave the old seven sided thrupenny pieces stacked up on the tables, which was quit profitable for me when clearing up after time, it used to supplement the seventeen shillings and sixpence pay I got quite nicely. We used to meet them at the Kenwood Swimming Pool, and were fascinated by them using "johnnies" (condoms!) *as they called them, as elastics to keep their trousers in their boot tops.*

At the top of the golf course (where the clubhouse now stands) *were tents where the "black yanks" as we called them were segregated and non-combatants we were told, when they went into town there was sometimes trouble and the MP's used to arrive with large batons. But all in all, they enjoyed good relations with the native population. Not knowing what the future held for them they always seemed to be able to enjoy themselves".*

* Lt. James Megellas (H Coy.) mentioned buying a bicycle in a letter home (taken from his excellent book "All the Way to Berlin" published by Presidio Press, March 2004). I guess there's a good chance it could have been from Francis's family bike shop:

"I am Battalion Officer of the Day today and I just finished checking the guard and guard posts. I used a bicycle to get around. Transport is scarce in this outfit since a parachute outfit is not authorized any vehicles, so over here a lot of the fellows have bought bikes. I bought one this-morning for seven pounds and ten shillings ($30.00). Most of the people here ride bikes. There are very few civilian cars."

Other 504 'troopers also purchased bicycles to get around. Terence Cartwright, a youngster at the time was very proud of his bicycle, which had been a birthday present from his mother, but couldn't resist the lure of the American's money!

"It was May 1944. A nice day, so I decided to visit and explore the ammunition dumps on the Barkby Thorpe Road followed by a quick check on the crop of fruit on a certain damson tree situated on Thorpe Farm, which we regularly 'scrumped'. I had just acquired for my birthday a bike for which my mother had paid, at great sacrifice, the sum of £3.10 shillings. This bike was purchased second hand from a local bike shop on the Green Lane Road and was a weird hybrid! - An adult frame with child's handlebars and odd size wheels - but to me it was my pride and joy liberating me from the confines of my local estate

It was when I neared the site of the aforesaid damson tree when I came across two rather large American soldiers who greeted me with 'hey son! Where's the

A 504 Paratrooper on his trusty steed!

Town?' On my answer that it was at least 3 miles away they asked me if they could buy my bike for £5.00! This represented a fortune to me, equal to at least 6 months spending money, so I quickly accepted their offer, and watched as these two 15 stone soldiers - one on the crossbar, set off - with shouts of 'Yippee' on an alarmingly wobbly downhill course towards Leicester.*

As I started my long walk home I began to have misgivings and wondered what my mother would say when she found out I had sold my birthday present. But I need not have worried, as when I arrived at the junction of Thurmaston Road I could not believe my eyes. There – indignantly thrown to one side of the road - was my bike. I found both tyres had burst and the front wheel was buckled! They had obviously decided to abandon the bike, as they were nowhere to be seen! I could not believe my luck! A few 'raids' on the council tip at Spence Street soon enabled me to get the bike back in running order, giving me constant use for the remainder of the war."

Pvt. Joe Blanchette

(*On this point Fred Baldino of A Company commented that money meant very little to them as they spent much of their time in combat, and didn't have any real opportunity to spend it. To illustrate this further, he recalls whilst the regiment was travelling through North Africa a friend, Joe Blanchette (left) light-heartedly suggested to him "lets rob the bank in this town", Fred responded, "Joe your Nuts, what the hell would we do with the money!").

Local boys bicycles were sometimes much in demand with some 504 'troopers; Local schoolboy John Collier explains:

"Paratroopers that had managed to get themselves in trouble would sometimes find themselves on punishment marches. These were led by a jeep, which if I remember rightly contained an officer and NCO's, whilst the men on punishment marched behind. When they were well away from the camp the jeep would return leaving the men to walk back. The funny part however was that the local lads & the men got together and after the jeep had returned the lads would cycle out and the men would hire the bikes from them and would cycle back leaving the bikes in the hedge a little way short of the camp for the lads to walk back and collect later".

John goes on to remember:

"I remember their time at Evington very well. I lived on Wakerley Road and they were always a great source of interest to me as a schoolboy growing up. I remember the coloured American labour units building the camp on the Leicestershire Golf Course on the site of what is now the clubhouse and the other one on Shady Lane at Evington. I also attended many of their services in St. Deny's Church at Evington and still have copies of some of their service sheets.

There was also a canteen in the corner of the Shady Lane Camp where the Shady Lane meets the Gartree Road. Some of the ladies from Evington including my mothers sister went there to help serve the men with Doughnuts & Coke, my first introduction to both as I went with my Aunt and the other ladies when they helped there. The doughnuts were cooked in another nearby tent by two paratrooper cooks Danny (who may have been an NCO) and a Pfc. J. Grieves. The canteen in the form of a large tent was under the direction of an American Red Cross lady Miss Louise Sheppard (she also had a very good voice & sang at some of their church services) who also had a tent close by for use when the men went on operations or exercises and movements in and out of the camp were banned.

We also learned that something special was to take place on the airfield at Stoughton (Leicester East) on 11th August 1944 but we had no idea what. We took picnics and walk up to the main entrance of the airfield it was obvious we were right by the amount of American traffic & after waiting quite a long while a convoy of MP's and a large staff car driven by a lady driver (Kay Summersby) containing General Eisenhower entered the camp.

I remember the American truck drivers seemed to have a problem negotiating the cross roads formed by Wakerley Road and Evington Lane. When they drove down from the direction of Evington (presumably from the Shady Lane camp) and turned left at the cross roads to enter the camp they kept knocking down a street light that stood on the corner. In the end after one such occasion, the Leicester corporation men replaced it and stood a paving kerbstone in front of it. The stone resembled a gravestone but to the best of my knowledge it was never knocked down again.

At this time Wakerley Road was a dead end and one day a group of about six boys acting rather suspiciously went up the road carrying something between them, and spent some time close to the hedge at the top of the road before running off. When they had left we went to see what they had been up to, and discovered a wooden box of American K rations that they had obviously "liberated". They had forced the lid off and run off with their pockets stuffed with as many rations as they could carry leaving the rest, which were soon cleared up by the residents who had gone to investigate the crime!

Whenever the Paratroopers made practice jumps just outside Leicester there was always a thriving trade amongst the local schoolboys in the ripcord handles from the emergency parachutes, and of other items that were left behind such as pilot chutes."

Barbara Elliott (now Brown) remembers wartime Oadby and the American Airborne troops (and General Ridgeway – right - checking up on 'his boys' behaviour):

"The American Airborne Troops, well one part of them, was stationed in the Church Hall, the Library and Swimming Pool in Oadby. They regularly gave the local children chewing gum; unheard of before the war.

We had a very popular Fish and Chip shop in the village, run by Mabel and Charley, no one ever referred to them by their surname. They sold wet fish during the day, but fried fish and chips in the evening Chips at 3 (old) pence and fish 6 (old) pence. The Americans loved their fish and chips and regularly used to queue with the locals and beg for the scratchings, as did the rest of us (scratchings being the bits of batter that used to fall off the fish).

One day, Charley painted on the shop window with whitewash: 'No Frying Tonight, No Fat', well the Americans were not going to be deprived of their fish and chips, so they supplied Mabel and Charley with a barrel of cooking oil so we could all have our delicacy. I was very young, but I was in the queue that evening and I

General Ridgeway takes time for a coffee with the American Red Cross whilst checking on "his boys" somewhere in Leicestershire.

remember Mabel confiding to an adult before me; 'we have never cooked with oil before'!!!

My sisters, Joan, Kathleen and I lived in a grocery shop in Oadby village run by my mother,

Bessie Elliott. My father, Irving Elliott was unfit for war service so worked in a munitions factory during the day, but drove ambulances for the ARP at nights! General Ridgeway, the American commander (18th Airborne Corps) called in the shop to ask my mother if the American troops were behaving themselves, which she was very pleased to say, they were. General Ridgeway was stationed in Sir Jonathan North's house (Glebe Mount, Glebe Road – left) opposite the Leicester Racecourse".

Katherine Goodwin from Oadby recalls that her father always kept a very neatly written diary, recording everything from family life to nation and world events. On March 5th 1944 he wrote *"walked up to Evington to see the American Camp and talk to the black soldiers"* (these GI's were obviously the labour battalion that set the camp up prior to the 504 arriving).

As 20 year old girls, Katherine and her friend Peggy loved to go dancing, and the De Montfort Hall in Leicester was their favourite venue. *"We would often dance together as most of our servicemen had gone away and there were few partners. Then, suddenly, Leicester seemed to be full of American GI's in their smart uniforms, and they too appeared in the dance halls around town. Naturally, we had 'dates', and eventually special friends. For myself, one of these was Staff Sergeant Frank Farmer of the 82nd Airborne Division, who was General Matthew Ridgeway's driver. He would call for me at home in a Jeep or sometimes the Generals Packard staff car.*

"On one occasion he bought a gift of cigarettes for my father, and one day left a large bag of freshly baked doughnuts for us. Frank would 'disappear' for days at a time, having been to the continent, Dad wrote in his diary on September 15th "Kay's paratrooper friends have gone away again (where?)", and on the 23rd – "visit from Frank and friend (driver and aide), back from Holland last night". Frank Farmer stayed with the General throughout the war and I was happy to discover that they survived and went back to the States together".

"Girls who went out with Americans were considered to be rather disloyal when our own boys were abroad, and indeed some did become involved with rather rough types, but in my experience my friends were extremely well mannered and gentlemanly, and my parents enjoyed welcoming them to our home and to meet our friends."

Mrs Primrose Hall, who was a young girl residing in Oadby during the war remembers a poem penned by she new not who, which while not directed specifically at the 504, takes a light-hearted look at the GI's in general in our midst at the time:

**Goddam Limey Jaywalkers - Now I's
gonna have tu shoot ma Jeep!!**

"Dear Old England's not the same,

We dreaded invasion when it came,

But now it's not the beastly Hun,

The God Damned Yankee Army's come,

We see them on the train and bus,

There isn't room for all of us,

We walk to let them have our seats,

And then get run-over by their Jeeps"!

I'm not certain what the original caption for the cartoon by American Stars and Stripes cartoonist Bill Mauldin was, or if indeed there was one, but the one added seems quite appropriate given the above poem!

Whilst on the subject of poems and such-like, it's worth mentioning that the Regiment had its own unofficial song, which tells of their exploits, this was penned by two English girls, M. BRADBURY and J. THURMAN, I'm not sure if they were from Leicester, but have no reason to believe otherwise, it was sung to the popular tune of the time "Lilly Marlene":

"We started out in Africa, many months ago,
Worked right up to Sicily, and then to Anzio,
There's where we showed them who we are,
The 504 won another Star,
Up with the 504 boys,
Up with the 504.

Then we went to England, just for a short rest,
The girls they sure did like us, we gave them all our best,
There in those dark and dismal streets,
The MP's walked their different beats,
But they couldn't stop the Airborne,
The fighting 504.

Then we got the orders, we got to jump next day,
Holland was the target, Oh what did Jerry say!!
There in our foxholes day and night,
We showed the huns just how to fight,
The jumpers of the Airborne,
The fighting 504,

The days that followed after, were spent in gay Paree,
Then we went to Belgium, and on to Germany,
And when the war is finally won,
They won't forget the deeds we've done,
Up with the 504 boys,
Up with the 504".

Chapter 2.

Home from Home – Comparatively Speaking.
(The 504 PIR in Leicestershire).

Once the paratroopers had settled in, time passed quickly. There were all sorts of recreational activities and sports to occupy their free time, as well as some tough training (after-all, there was a war on!), and even a little leave. Boots had been spit-polished to perfection. You could just about have shaved using their boots as mirrors, and the knife-edge creases that ran down the length of each paratrooper's bloused trouser legs as a razor. The old inter-regimental rivalries that had been the cause of so many black eyes and fat lips in the past were forgotten for the moment. 504 men actually shook hands with their "brothers in arms" in the 505 (who were billeted at Quorne, north of Leicester) and they drank beer together in the numerous pubs in town.

There were at least two issues of a regimental news-sheet entitled "The Panel" printed and distributed throughout the regiment in May 1944. This consisted of an 8¼ inch by 14 inch sheet printed on both sides. It's not known if subsequent issues were printed, or indeed who published numbers one and two. Reported in Vol. 1 No. 2 was news of some leave (furloughs) in London:

<u>504th PARATROOPERS TO HAVE FURLOS – THREE DAYS, TWO NIGHTS IN LONDON.</u>

Furlough passes will be issued to men of the 504th Parachute Infantry, it was stated today by Lieutenant Hauptfleisch, 504th Regimental Adjutant.

Lieutenant Hauptfleisch said that the furloughs will be limited to three days and that the men will be obliged to spend their furloughs in the City of London. This restriction is necessitated by an Army directive which asserts that every man, in order to be eligible for an overnight pass or furlough, must have a positive reservation for sleeping quarters made in advance of the issuance of the pass. Since it would be impossible for most of us to make the required reservations, the 82nd division has reserved billets at the American Red Cross in London for those 504th men on furlough.

- Three Hour Trip -

London is three hours from Leicester by rail and four special trains will leave Leicester at approximately one hour intervals commencing at 08:15 hours.

The furlough passes will be issued as soon as the service records arrive and payroll can be made out. The service records are expected to come in today and a partial payment will be made as promptly thereafter as possible. About ten percent of the regiment will be given furloughs at one time.

S/Sgt David Rosenkrantz was one of those lucky enough to go on leave during August 1944, and the following letter describes amongst other things his experience of the Great British seaside!

"Dear folks,

Well, I guess you are all anxious to hear about where I went on my furlough. I went to a city in the northwest of England that is known as the "Coney Island" of England. It is a regular beach resort and has just about everything that a beach should have except good weather and Americans to give it the right atmosphere. It is funny as hell to see all the people leave the beach at the same time

S/Sgt David Rosenkrantz (left) and Pvt . Louis Holt of H Coy. at Shady Lane camp. (photo courtesy of Phil Rosenkrantz)

to go home to eat lunch, exactly at twelve, coming back at the same time, then all leaving to go home to tea at the same time. You can just about tell what time it is by the way the people are going to or from the beach. The weather is no good for swimming, too cold and foggy, get about a couple of hours of sunshine in the afternoon about nine o'clock. I had a pretty good time though. Took life easy, and really relaxed like I intended to. I want to thank Harry for sending the money to me. It didn't get here in time as I expected, but I managed to borrow the fifty bucks in the meantime so it didn't really matter too much but we would have all been in a pretty bad way if the army hadn't arranged things so that the boys could write checks in a bank in town on the accounts that they had at home. Probably be a lot of rubber checks bouncing around here soon but I don't think anyone is really worried about them, least of all the guys that wrote them. I forgot to tell you the name of the beach, it's "Blackpool" not what you'd expect the name of a beach to be, Huh?

Received a letter from Goldie yesterday of July 22. Says she is takin' a rest under doctors' orders. Well, I hope she is better now. She better take a nice long rest for me now. Last night we were out on one of those nasty night problems again. This time we were out on one of those English moors that I always read about but never saw. It is part of the country that a heavy fog always hangs over so that the grass is always wet and the ground swampy. In a little while our feet and legs were soaking wet and cold. Go out of sight of everyone in the fog and you're lost? And I do mean lost. If we didn't have a compass we'd walk round in circles. One fellow came back to the same place twice in ten minutes and each time he thought he was going in a straight line. Really a fog!

That's about it for now. All my love to Ma and Pa and all the rest. Goldie still like the Scotchman? So long now -- be good.

David"

(S/Sgt. Rosenkrantz was subsequently posted as Missing in Action in Holland on 27th September 1944. In recent years it has come to light after much research by his family that he was setting up an outpost in a farmhouse by the Den Heuvel woods when a German counter-attack occurred through the woods. The 504 men were cut off and surrounded. S/Sgt Rosenkrantz was standing behind a tree and was shot from behind by a machine gun. The other trooper in the picture above, Pvt. Louis Holt was killed in action several days earlier whilst taking part in the famous crossing of the River Waal at Nijmegen in Holland).

Pfc. Bonnie Roberts has the following memories of England:

"We went from Naples to England with the Capetown Castle. It was full and loaded. We landed at Liverpool and we moved to Leicester. That was where we were training (and the 505 was training at Nottingham). I primarily remember Leicester as we trained up there. We made a few jumps and maintained our status".

One such practice jump was code-named 'Operation Bumblebee'. Unfortunately on the day an irregular directional wind was blowing about the drop zone, and one Sergeant Albert Clark of A Company landed astride a hedge whilst attempting to cope with it and hurt his back. The Medical Officer suggested that an old fashioned hot bath should ease the pain and help effect a cure. Sadly the camp only had showers, but his girl friend, Kathleen, a local girl came to the rescue and Albert soothed his aching muscles in a bath at her parent's home in nearby Oadby. Albert returned to Oadby in 1946 and married Kathleen in the village church (St. Peters) and took her back to California.

Sergeant Clark recalls the Shady Lane site, how he met Kathleen, and the fateful parachute jump:

"Shady Lane in Evington was to be our regimental home for the next 5 or 6 months, and was located about 4 miles from the city centre of Leicester, which had a population of about 350,000 and was a very rich industrial area. There were all kinds of entertainment and the people were really very friendly. For the first two weeks we were held in quarantine and not allowed to leave the camp area. Our quarters were 5 or 6 man tents amongst some trees and it was very nice. The one thing we had a hard time getting used to was bed check at 11:00 p.m., when you could sit outside the tent and read a newspaper as it was still so light. They (the British) *were on double daylight saving time and we were so far north that at times when on night manoeuvres you could make out a person at 100 yards or so in the wee hours of the morning. But the training went well and so did the fraternizing with the public. It was the best duty that most of us had enjoyed since being in the service, even in the States.*

The second night I went to town and was at a dance, I was looking for Sergeant Milt Knight. When I eventually found him, he and another man, Sergeant John Kessler of Headquarters Company were talking to three girls. I was introduced and took care of the little business I had with Milt. The orchestra was on a short break and when they started playing again, Milt and John each took a partner and left the third girl and me standing there. Milt had taken a few steps, when he turned and came back and said, "All right, you two are properly introduced. Now don't let this music go to waste". So the rest of the evening didn't go to waste. The other two girls were sisters that Milt and John had met earlier. The three girls worked together and were on what they called fire watch, where they worked. We got along very well and I spent most of my spare time with Kathleen and her family that summer.

The day of the jump when I got hurt wasn't a particularly windy day, just a little breezy and there was an irregular directional breeze. We jumped at about 600 feet and I changed directions about 5 times. I was trying to clear a hedge and expected to hit a ditch between the hedge and the road when the wind took me back across the hedge. I had my feet in my hip pockets when I hit the fence on the field side. I was in a V position – my feet in the air on one side and my hand in the air on the other side.

I hit the ground on my tail bone, the second time on my back with my feet over my head, and the third time I hit the ground my left arm was under me, I was on my left shoulder and left side of my face. I laid there for a while before I could get out of my harness, gather my gear and join the rest of the platoon.

We crossed the road and waited for orders of where to go. It was about 1 or 2 minutes before we moved off. We went back across the road and I got through the first fence and straddled the second fence and I couldn't go either way, and it took several men to get me out of there. They tagged me and left me to be picked up and taken to hospital.

The Battalion Surgeon (Captain Charles Zirkle) looked me over and said that he would send me back to camp as all they would do at the hospital would be to put a piece of plywood under the mattress and let me lay there. I gradually worked myself back to getting around, for about three weeks I waddled like a duck!"

On another jump, Captain Adam Komosa (HQ & HQ Company) led his men out of the door of the leading C47. His parachute started oscillating violently in the wind, and he was unable to control it before he hit the ground. The subsequent force with which he landed rendered him completely paralysed from the neck down (luckily for him only temporarily). As he laid helplessly in the Drop Zone other C-47's flew overhead dropping their sticks of paratroopers. Some of their equipment, such as weapons and helmets, broke loose and showered down on those below. Captain Komosa looking up could see the danger, and as other paratroopers struggled out of their harnesses warnings were being shouted. "Look out! M-1 (rifle) coming down!" but there was little he could do. The weapon plunged into the ground not far from his shoulder, and buried itself right up to the trigger guard. He then spent several weeks laid up in hospital until he learnt of operation Market Garden in Holland. He was determined that he would not be left behind, but the Medical Officers had banned him from parachuting for six months. So he arranged to go in by glider, (probably with the 325th Glider Infantry Regiment which was billeted at nearby Scraptoft) acting as a co-pilot.

Oops!!

On the 21st May 1944 the Tomlinson family of Barkby Thorpe were celebrating their son Norman's 21st birthday, and recall in the early evening seeing a practice jump of approximately 2500 US Paratroopers over Hamilton Farm.

At least one other practice jump appears that it might have been made at night. The exercise took place on the night of the 19/20th June when according to notes made by Staff Sgt. Daun Z. Rice of 2nd platoon, H Company (pictured left), they were to jump over the villager of Burton Overy at 24:00hrs. Burton Overy for the purpose of the exercise was held by a Ranger Division, also one regiment of an Anti-Parachute unit were in the vicinity of Market Harborough (spelled with a 'B' in his notes). The 3rd Division were apparently coming in from the North West, and the 504 were to jump at 24:00hrs and prevent the enemy from

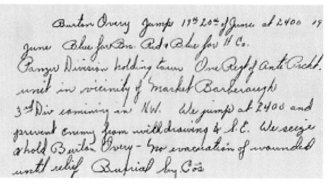

Notes taken by Sgt. Rice referring to a night exercise at Burton Overy.

withdrawing to the South East. They were to seize and hold Burton Overy. There was to be no evacuation of the wounded until relief arrived.

18

Staff Sgt. Rice, like many of the 504 paratroopers was obviously popular with the local girls. I have on record two of his girlfriend's addresses in Leicester; one was on Osborne Road, and the other on Ripon Street. Sadly, also like many others, he was subsequently killed in action (on the 26th of September 1944) during Operation Market Garden.

Hugh Gibbs, a local farm worker, witnessed another mass practice jump in late August:

"I think it was on August 25th, I was stooking wheat (the corn was cut and tied by a machine called a binder then they would be picked up by hand and put in the shape of an A, 6 or 8 at a time to make a 'stook'). I was in a field overlooking the Welland Valley (east of Market Harborough) when I heard the Dakota transport planes coming. It was a fantastic sight when 2,200 American parachutists dropped about half a mile away."

Pfc. Darrell Harris of Hq & Hq Company recalled one practice jump where they landed so far off the intended Drop Zone that they ended up having to take a train ride back to Leicester!

Lt. Reneau Breard of A Company recalls other night exercises in the surrounding area:

"We carried out several manoeuvres at night in the fields around Great Glen, Little Stretton, Kings Norton, and Illston on the Hill. I never knew if any of the local people complaining of the noise we made, but I'm sure they were relieved when we finally left on 17th September".

The 504 on one of several parades through Leicester.

Generally speaking, life settled into something of a routine, although it did seem on occasions as if it was one big parade after another, with the men of the 504 saluting the British, the British returning the complement (and everyone's feet getting tired!). It would appear however that the paratrooper's efforts did not go un-noticed, as they impressed the local citizens around Leicester and British Army Officers with there snappy turn-out; the following report appeared in the regimental news sheet "The Panel".

504TH ACCLAIMED BY LEICESTER AS BEST, AWOLS THE LEAST EVER – "BONO"

The versatile 504th Parachute Infantry donned its OD Blouses for the first time in over a year and on their first trip to Leicester was credited by citizens, British Officers, and impartial Americans with being the snappiest appearing and best behaved army unit to hit the city.

With the exception of one or two isolated cases, there were no delinquencies. At the end of the first and up until we go to press there has been reported but one case of AWOL, and it consisted of nothing more serious than being thirty minutes late.

Major Wellems (right), who is a stickler for Military courtesy and appearance, and no one to pay a compliment where it is not due, observed that the men of the 504th out saluted and out shone every other unit in the city. "The healthiest, sharpest looking bunch of men I've seen", he said. Definitely "Bono".

Prior to the "take off" men could be seen throughout the camp polishing boots, ironing wrinkled trousers with heated mess kits, devising hangers for blouses from bits of bailing wire, sewing on insignias, shaving, showering and in a hundred ways preparing for their English debut. From all reports it was highly successful.

One "Bobby" standing on duty near the old clock tower remarked about the class cut appearance of the "new" paratroopers; "I've seen thousands of soldiers both British and American, but of all I've ever seen none looked as spoony as you boys, you're proper generals".

There was training during the day, but in the evening and during off duty periods there were passes to be had, and they weren't difficult to get. Even if you couldn't get a pass (and weren't prepared to go AWOL over the wall!), with regular movies, sports, a well-stocked day room, and Louise's "doughnut dugout", it was just about possible to spend an enjoyable night on camp.

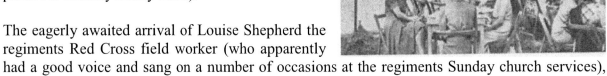

The 'dugout catered for everything from full-blown tea parties, as seen in the picture right, too a two-minute shampoo! (I believe that the hedge and double tree line apparent at the back of the picture is actually Shady Lane).

The eagerly awaited arrival of Louise Shepherd the regiments Red Cross field worker (who apparently had a good voice and sang on a number of occasions at the regiments Sunday church services), was reported thus in "The Panel" news sheet:

COMING! – THE DAILY DUNKING HOUR PLUS ONE DONUT MACHINE PLUS ONE GIRL.

We don't know her name yet, but commencing tomorrow, unless the unforeseen occurs, and it usually does, donuts will be dispensed by hands fairer than those of any mess sergeant who ever slapped a meat streaked slab of greasy fat into a steel cold mess kit.

As we said, her name is still a mystery, but what is important is not the name, but the fact that she's a "she". Our Red Cross girl will become a permanent institution at Camp Stoughton, working herself to pieces during the day making donuts, and serving them nightly between the hours of 1920 and 2100 with a mixture of coffee and bewitching charm.

If foxholes have made you cynical and you are inclined to be sceptical, keep your eyes peeled for a complicated mass of shinning steel, valves and knobs. That will be the donut machine. It is expected to arrive momentarily. Miss? should be within a sigh and a whistle of it.

According to a late breaking piece of news in the second edition of "The Panel", those who were sceptical and cynical have good reason to be:

SOME LAST MINUTE DOPE ON THE DONUT DUGOUT.

There are several last minute statements to be made in connection with the donut machine and the donut girl that we so glibly announced in our first issue was on the way.

Firstly there will be no chromium plated, diamond studded donut machine. Miss? will have to make the donuts by the more primitive and less spectacular method.

Secondly, the inevitable has happened and our donut girl has been unavoidably detained. Apparently the delay is being caused by the lack of supplies. (Ed. Note: It takes a lot of dough, sugar, etc. to keep this outfit in donuts each day.) Besides, we don't want a donut girl without any donuts. Or do we?

The following memory of this time was taken from a document written by Pvt. Eddie Livingston entitled "The first time I saw Paris" (Eddie was subsequently taken prisoner in Normandy on 9th June 1944).

"The 504th was bivouacked near-by-to a golf course, near-by-to Leicester, England. The greens were lush with blue-green grass, upon which fat milk cows grazed placidly. There were many emerald green meadows, tiny garden plots, quaint stone buildings all about us, reminding one of a children's play-land. But the things I remember best about England were the honey-pots! (It would be inappropriate and superfluous to go into greater details about the honey-pots!)" – The golf course remains to this day, but I doubt that you would see cows grazing on the greens now!

Sgt. Tallons' memories of the regiment's time in England are as follows (taken from Moffatt Burriss' excellent book Strike and Hold published by Potomac Books: August 2000):

"The Capetown Castle docked at Liverpool, England, on 22 April 1944. Jolly Old England! What a wonderful place to be after leaving battle-scarred Anzio. It was wonderful to be back in an area of the world where we weren't constantly on the alert for an enemy attack. Our troops left Liverpool about 2300 that night for the city of Leicester. Our training and routine were light there. We were allowed to move around and become acquainted with the country and the people – especially the girls. After what we'd been through, the girls seemed beautiful. They were nice to us, and lots of fun to be with.

I was just a country boy from Dillon, South Carolina, who couldn't dance and had no opportunity to learn. However, I saw that troopers who could dance had a much better time than those of us who couldn't. So one evening I sailed out on the floor and danced. I still love to dance, and fortunately, I'm a much better dancer now.

One Afternoon a buddy and I were riding our bicycles, and we saw two girls playing tennis. So we wheeled in and started getting acquainted. The girl I met that afternoon has been a friend since 1944. My wife and I have been to England to see her, and she has visited the States to see us. Recently, she retired from a very exciting and demanding job with Exxon International.

In some ways, the troopers were more fortunate than the English civilians. One day at camp, the mess hall served Salisbury steak. Since a number of the troopers were away, there was a lot of food left over. I had made friends with an English family named Wright. They were Catholic, and had eight children. When I saw all this uneaten food, I thought of this family and asked the mess sergeant for some of the leftovers. He immediately agreed and helped me pack the meals. Then, as I headed for their house, I wondered if the Wrights would be offended. They were not!

Mrs. Wright told me that what I took to them that day was more meat than they were allowed to buy in a month. She thanked me again each time we saw each other."

To the paratroopers the city of Leicester was great; it definitely wasn't a 'fast' town. There were no 'honky-tonks', dives, or even a half decent nightclub like "back home", but there were dance halls like the Corn Exchange in the Market Place, the De Montfort Hall where very often the 504 Parachute Swing Band (who's theme tune was "Sentimental Journey") provided the entertainment, and the wonderful jitterbug paradise The Palais de Dance on Humberstone

The Corn Exchange in the Market Place, Leicester

The 504 Parachute Swing Band onstage at De Montfort Hall, Leicester. (Photo courtesy of Deryk Wills)

Gate. (Ah yes, the "Pally", now I could tell you one or two stories about that particular establishment, for I used to frequent the place in the early to mid 1970's myself; 30 years after the guys from the 504, but I guess with pretty much the same thing on my mind - girls!!). Yes, there were girls aplenty (I originally thought this is what Eddie Livingston was referring to when he talked about "the honey-pots", although another veteran, Fred Baldino has since suggested that this was a reference to the somewhat less appealing cans used in the chemical toilets on the camp – the men who had to clean these out were known as "Honey Dippers").

Anyway, back to the girls; there were pretty ones, who wore saddle shoes, swing skirts and sweaters like their American counterparts. There were intelligent girls, dumb girls, classy girls, plain girls, rich girls and poor girls. There was a girl for every man and one didn't have to look

A "Jitterbug Paradise". The Palais on Humberstone Gate. (Photograph by courtesy of the Leicester Mercury).

too far either. The English girls proved a pleasant surprise to the American boys, who had been brought up to believe that British females were flat-chested, pale-cheeked, lank haired and very reserved! A night in the "Pally", (where loose-hipped lithe-footed girls renovated the paratroopers' jitterbug steps that had been half forgotten whilst up in the Italian mountains), soon dispelled any preconceived notions about British female reserve. The only noticeable difference between the British girls and their American counterparts was that in England they called the dance a "quick step".

The Panel news-sheet of May 1, 1944, reported amongst other things that the 504's next "jump" was to be at the De Montfort Hall! (Pictured above right – taken in 1940):

504TH MEN, five hundred strong, will swing away on May 9th at the De Montfort Hall, Leicester to the strains of two fifteen piece bands at the first of a series of regimental dances scheduled for the enlisted men of the unit.

The Auxiliary Territorial Service (ATS), five hundred of them too, with boots shined, red lips and hair upswept, will attend on masse in order that each paratrooper might have what it takes to fill the demands of a "hot lick", fox trot, waltz, or whatever form the art of "tripping the light fantastic" currently makes in Merry England.

Refreshments, consisting mainly of beer, will be sold at the bar. Cold cuts and sandwiches will also be available for those couples whose efforts on the dance floor become frenzied enough to

Men of the 504 with their partners on the dance floor at Leicester's De Montfort Hall.

rouse an appetite.

There will be an admission charge of two shillings and sixpence (fifty cents) for each man. It is suggested that because of the limited capacity of the hall, that you start bucking now for your reservation. The affair, aside from being the grandest of its kind since the 504th has been overseas, holds promise of opening many new lines of endeavour for those men fortunate enough to be present. Be there if you can. However, if you're pulling guard and can't get away, take consolation in the knowledge that this is only the first of several similar events planned for the men of the 504th. In order to insure that the mixed assemblage of girls and paratroopers be perfectly and harmoniously divisible by two, men will be asked to refrain from bringing dates.

There was also a late update regarding this event in Vol.1 No.2 (dated May 3rd 1944) of The Panel:

"600 TO ATTEND MAY 9TH DANCE INSTEAD OF 500."

A recalculation of the capacity of the De Montfort Hall, Leicester, has resulted in a revision of the original number of men planned to go to the dance. An extra one hundred paratroopers (and an equal number of ATS girls) can be accommodated now. Beer will be sold at the bar and there will be something to eat either cold cuts or sandwiches or possibly both.

Local newspaper, The Leicester Mercury carried a report on one of several dances at De Montfort Hall:

AMERICANS GUESTS OF LORD MAYOR.

Leicester was privileged to entertain representatives of American fighting units and members of British Women's Services. A pleasant and peaceful "off-duty" evening was spent by about 1000 guests of the Lord Mayor and Lady Mayoress (Councillor and Mrs. C.E. Gillot) in the charmingly decorated De Montfort Hall, banked with flowers and hung with flags.

Despite the fact that Leicester's chief citizens had been entertaining since three o'clock in the afternoon, they willingly stood with 53 American representatives - soldiers from every corner of the United States to be pictured by "Leicester Mercury" photographers for despatch to each of the States.

N.F.S. girls were among W.A.A.F and A.T.S members many of whom renewed acquaintance with American partners who had attended an earlier Allied Forces Party. An attractive blonde in Air Force Blue, Corporal Lille Metcalfe, and a little Scottish Corporal from Stirlingshire, both agreed that evenings such as these were "good for morale, and a treat for the deserving W.A.A.F"!

An American was heard to remark that if he won a certain handsomely dressed doll, it was destined for a trip to Berlin! The doll, with a silk embroidered nightdress case, was eventually won by a hefty American Officer from Pennsylvania. Lieu. Monty Pearson regarded his unexpected prize with great affection and informed his friends that he would promptly despatch it across the Atlantic to his mother.

State representative for Louisiana was T/S Tony Cascio (23), whose family are well-known in his home town of Monroe. They keep "Cascio's" the grocery store on Oak Street, where Tony spent his working days before joining the forces. "England is the closest place to home I hope to find" he said.

A former screw factory worker from Providence, Pvt. Louis Costa (21) represented Rhode Island. "I think Leicester is a pretty good place" he grinned. His Portuguese parents went over to the States, where they became American citizens, and settled in Providence to bring up a family of four boys and four girls, of whom Louis is the eldest.

A noted song writer from the States was caught humming a line or two for his next song. Carl Sigman, looking fit and well, confessed to being the author of "Pennsylvania Six Five Thousand", a popular jazz number, which was Glenn Miller's identification tune while staying at the well-known Hotel Pennsylvania." He also wrote "Love Lies" and "Busy as a Bee", among others which have gained success over here, and has done much night club work for

George White, the producer. Carl Sigman, who is from Brooklyn N.Y., wrote his first song for a show at New York University, were he studied not music, but law, and gained his degree! At present he is helping to produce a show with American, A.T.S., and civilian artists, the complete score being written by him. One of the biggest songs of the show is "England made me feel at Home" he said, and that's how we all feel.

Another admirer of Leicester was a boxer, Emmett Yanez, of St. Paul, Minnesota, who has three other brothers fighting, one in New Guinea.

Dance music was provided by a military band, which has played for many social functions since leaving America. They're only waiting now to introduce their latest jazz numbers to a conquered German capital. After the final "Grand March" led by the Lord Mayor and Lady Mayoress to

the rousing tune of the American Airborne Song, dancers stood in silence for the "Star Spangled Banner" and "God Save the King". Thus completing yet another link in the Anglo-American chain.

Reported in the same issue of the Panel was a Company B dance in Wigston.

"FIRST COMPANY DANCE RATED A BIG SUCCESS.

"Last night at Constitutional Hall, Wigston, a medley of two hundred ATS girls and Company B Paratroopers kept the dance floor rocking to a rhythm provided by the 82nd

Constitution Hall, Wigston, venue for Company B's dance in early May 1944.

Division Artillery Band. The dance was unquestionably a success. Beer was served, though of course not nearly enough. However, nobody seemed to mind particularly, for the girls were deluxe and dancing to the Artillery Band (they played while we ate doughnuts yesterday) was strictly an A1 activity.

It was noted that Sergeant "old man" Glover kicks a mean toe, despite the fact that there is something about his fox trotting that is vaguely reminiscent of the plowman.

In a letter home dated 17th April 1944 (just prior to the 504's arrival, but indicative of the time), Charlotte Colburn, an American Red Cross worker attached to the 82nd Airborne Division who later became a firm favourite with the men of the 504, comments on Leicester's nightlife:

"They have here where I am now a dance hall called the "Palais de Danse" - most popular with all our boys and quite large. There are always more English girls than there are boys, however, and contrary to our traditions - the girls do the cutting in - not the boys. Girls here dance together - particularly jitterbug - a great deal. The pay off was a little incident that occurred Saturday night. Anne and I were wandering about town with our dates trying to scrape up something to do. Anne is our new girl who was with a darling 2nd Lt. called Pinky because his last name is Salmon and he has red hair and I was with John Thurner - Yale - that I have mentioned before. Everything here starts about 6 o'clock, movies, dance halls, pubs etc., and we never get around until 8 - too late for movies - the beer is all gone by 9 - h--- of a mess. Sooo we wandered into the ballroom of the Bell Hotel, which was crowded with dancers - British (army and civilian) and a scattering of American Officers as usual. The band – 5 pieces - played by old decrepit Englishmen with just about an ounce of spark left, was throwing out such new and modern things as "Honeysuckle Rose" and murdering them. Before each dance they hold up a

little sign to tell you what it is going to be - waltz, rumba quick step, etc. - this is because you could never tell from the music itself. As we stood there taking in the situation with our superior American attitudes showing slightly, an American Officer danced by with an English girl and at that moment a British girl cut in on the officer as she wished to dance with her girl friend, leaving our Officer - the poor dear - stranded and definitely embarrassed in the middle of the floor. That is one for the books don't you think? We danced for the rest of the evening and probably looked just as funny as the rest - but, oh, we don't think so".

Ross Carter wrote in his book "Those Devils in Baggy Pants" (first published in 1950):

"When the British girls in Leicester and adjoining towns learned that one of the crack outfits of the American Army was close by and that we hadn't kissed an English-speaking girl since 1943, they moved in on us like Dakota grasshoppers on a garden patch in a drought year. The sweet rosy-cheeked darlings swamped to the confines of our camp by bicycle, pony-cart, taxi, and on foot, and hung over the fence to sheep's-eye us. The guard around the fences had to be doubled to prevent our leaping them and taking off before class "A" uniforms could be found for us. We drooled, pawed the ground, and shook the fences!

(Local youngster Michael Wilford, who was then 9 years old recalls seeing large numbers of young [and not so young] women hanging around the camp; at the time, he could not understand what the attraction was!)

Within six weeks, pregnant women began coming into the regimental personnel section, wanting the erring jokers ('troopers) to marry them or at least to make an allotment of a pound a week for sixteen years for the upbringing of the ripening love fruit. At the end of sixteen years, the youngster would presumably be large enough to forage for its own living. The erring lovers roared and bellowed at the thought of being penalized financially over so long a time for what they regarded as a trifling matter!"

Gerald Salmon of South Knighton recalls various "antics" going on between the American GI's and local girls:

"When our parents were not around, local kids of all sorts of ages felt it appropriate to swagger around in front of the GI's with a fag dangling from their mouths, chewing gum, since that was what Hollywood had convinced us Americans did. The presence of the GI's, and their well-publicised generosity attracted young women (and some not so young), from all over the City and some of the antics we did see gave us an insight into the facts of life long before our due time. It did provide mirth and amusement for all of us and our tree climbing skills very often gave us privileged sights of frolics we should not be witnessing!"

There were also numerous pubs around, and they could drink all the (warm!) British beer they could hold (and if you got to be a regular at the Crown and Thistle it was rumoured that you could even get drunk on spirits!). The Queens, the Royal Oak, the Swan with Two Necks, the Imperial Hotel and dozens of other pubs were all well frequented by the men of the 504.

Pictured here are 504 Paratroopers parading through Leicester passed the strangely named "Swan with Two Necks" public house on Granby Street which was a popular watering hole for the American Paratrooper's. (As a matter of interest, the history behind this pubs rather strange name goes back to the reign of Elizabeth I. Swans have traditionally been the property of the reigning Monarch in England, but Elizabeth I granted the right to ownership of some swans to the Worshipful Company of Vintners. In order to be able to tell which Swan belonged to whom, it was decided that Vintners' swans should have their beaks marked with two notches, or nicks. In those days, 'neck' was another form of the word 'nick' so the Vintners spotted that a Swan with Two Necks could afford them a rather clever pun, and a striking pub sign).

The Haunch of Venison (now The Orange Tree – the picture on the left shows the pub as it is

today) on High Street was the established gathering place of those who followed the fight game in Leicester, and it was there that boxing matches between American and British paratroopers were organized.

Interestingly, I can remember my father telling stories of the "unofficial fights" (alcohol fuelled brawls at throwing out time one suspects!) that used to take place between these two groups, especially at the Royal Oak, where, as young teenagers, my father and his friends saw these events as the highlight of a Saturday evenings entertainment!

The Imperial Hotel

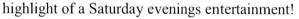

28

Pfc. Arvil Webster of E Company (left) was wounded in Italy, and shipped out to North Africa to recover. He arrived in Leicester in early June a month or so after the rest of the regiment, with four other troopers who had also been wounded. He remembers some happy times in Leicester where he found the local people were mostly very kind and friendly. He recalls making a couple of practice jumps, and some combined training with British Paratroopers from the 1st Airborne Division, who were also billeted around the county. According to Pfc. Webster some "unofficial exercises" also took place between these two Units in some of the towns pubs, with "*Minor Scuffles*" breaking out – usually caused by arguments over which unit was the toughest (typical Airborne troops Espree D' Corps). Apparently it required a not unsubstantial number of MP's to separate the two sides on these occasions!

Pfc. Webster was subsequently wounded again in Holland during the Market Garden operation and spent two years in hospital recovering from his injuries.

The Panel news-sheet had a section entitled "Sport Shorts" written by Bill Bridgeman where the Regiments 'legitimate' sporting activities and achievements were reported. Boxing received its fair share of column inches. From Vol. 1 No.1 we have the following:

SPORTS SHORTS.

"BOXING"

"I see where some of our prominent pugs have taken up their favourite pastime again. Though it is perhaps a bit late, Dave Farrier is to be congratulated for his fine showing in the 5th Army Boxing Tournament held in Italy some time ago. Let's see more of it Dave.

A few of the other boxers who are worth watching are Boaz of D company, George Sylvasy of G company, Sergeant Murphy of B company, and Red Murdock of 3rd Bn".

The 504 Regimental Boxing Team.

America's national sport, Baseball also got its fair share of page space, as did other sports such as tennis, and even table tennis, although I'm not sure the motive on this occasion was purely sporting!

"There's been some talk of organizing a table tennis tournament with the winner to play the champion of the ATS (you know those grey-green stockings from the other side of town). This is a darn good suggestion and a fine example of the ends to which a paratrooper will go in order to foster a relationship with the fair sex. I wonder if the ATS does go in for table tennis – hm, I used to be a fair hand at the game myself."

Golf was also included in Vol.1 No.2:

"Here's a morsel that ought to be of interest to some of you golf starved divot diggers. Sergeant Sam D'Crenza (left), Headquarters Company, 1st Battalion, and former golf pro of Westchester County, New York, is looking into the possibilities of organizing a golf club. The map says that we're situated smack in the middle of a golf course, which fact, of course, means nothing to duffers and sports alike if there are no putters, mashies, drivers, etc. forthcoming.

However, Sam, who is a convincing talker, hopes that he might be able to persuade some of the local patrons of the sport to lend their clubs to the boys that would like to play. We don't know how it will work out, but if anyone can swing it Sam can".

Staff Sgt. Gerard W. Valles of G Company ran the 3rd Battalion Softball team:

"1st Sgt. W. C. Long of G Company who knew me from back in the States, asked me to be the Manager of the Battalion Softball Team; the way he put it, it wasn't exactly an order, but more than just a request! We arranged with several of the Company teams that played each other to put together a pretty good Battalion team. We were all enlisted men on the teams, although the Officers usually showed up on game day to cheer their men on. We held quite a few practice games in the field just past I Company area at Camp Stoughton. One bonus of being involved with the team was that we were able to avoid some of the extra duties that accompanied army garrison life.

The first real game we played was against an Air Force team from one of the airfields nearby, I don't recall the unit, but we gave them a solid walloping. Then we played a team of British soldiers who had never played Softball before. Needless to say we beat them but they were good sports and we all laughed and had a good time. It almost made us forget the people we left behind in Anzio. It was a time to enjoy

Despite the title, this photo is of one of the 504's Softball teams (judging by the size of the ball) – possibly even S/Sgt. Valles' 3rd Battalion team. It was taken at Evington Playing Fields on 31st August, and appeared in the Leicester Evening Mail newspaper on 1st September 1944.

for we new it was just a brief respite.

We received an invitation to play cricket from a local civilian team. The game was to be played in the evening and no one in our battalion wanted to participate, (our evenings off were for social activities in town as far as we were concerned, and not to be given up lightly!) However, we didn't want to lose face and be called "no shows", so Sgt. Long told me I could use the guys who were in the stockade on restrictions for one reason or another (I was also on restrictions for a minor infraction at the time!) The game turned out to be a shocker, Paul Taylor from G Company knew how to hit a long ball. He batted for a half an hour, and the outcome was we beat them. I still remember how they cheered and applauded us.

There was a pub in Leicester called "The White Swan". It became the meeting place for the 504 guys and the British Paratroopers from the 6th Airborne Division. They weren't crazy about all

Organised sport however was not to everyone's taste, and some just preferred to take it easy during their off duty periods!

Yanks, but if you were with the 504 you had a friend for life. We fought side by side with them in Italy, and would soon be doing so in Holland.

A crazy silly thing we would do was to string imaginary wire all over Leicester. You would be walking in town with a young lady and she would suddenly stop and tell you "look out for that wire" they went along with our charade and laughed with us. In Italy they never caught on to it.

Anyway, September soon came around and we left for Holland. About 30 days into the fighting there we learned we would not be returning to Leicester and the UK. This was not very well received by most of the troopers as most if not all had made some good friends in Leicester, and those of us who survived still have fond memories of our time in the UK. Many of us corresponded with friends they made for years after the war. Some of us went back. It was a happy time during a tough period for both soldiers and civilians. I still cherish those memories."

Following on from S/Sgt. Valles mention of Cricket, an article appeared in the Leicester Mercury newspaper in May 1944 entitled "AMERICANS AT CRICKET" (written by Mr. Leicester who still has a column today!), which whilst not a commentary of this particular game did pose one or two questions:

"I am interested in seeing how the fact that Americans in England are now playing cricket affects the future of the sport. Our transatlantic friends have in the course of history taken a good many sports from us, and sometimes transformed them as in the cases of Rounder's, Americanised into Baseball, and Rugby Football, and others which they have preserved unchanged and virtually internationalised – lawn tennis and golf. What will they do – if anything – with cricket? I am pretty sure that if they go on with it, they will not leave this game unchanged. In the past, transatlantic visitors have been pretty scornful about cricket: they have described it as a rite rather than a game. Compared with Baseball it is undeniably "slow", but it may be that the finer points of it will eventually appeal. International games, in which America would make a third with England and Australia, are a possibility."

Of course, sixty odd years later, we have not seen the uptake optimistically suggested by the columnist, I guess "the finer points" never did appeal!

The Americans love of sport was inevitably responsible for a number of romantic relationships.

 Doreen Scholes who lived on Dunton Street, Leicester was a young girl whose place of work was near to the Shady Lane site in Evington. She was cycling home from work one day when she saw a group of Yanks playing baseball. She was curious about the mechanics of the game so she stopped to observe. One of the Paratroopers who were watching the game, Sgt. William Kline of C Company (left - from Kent Ohio) saw her and the two struck up a conversation. He explained as best he could, how the game was played. The two seemed to hit it off and William asked Doreen if she would show him some of the historic statues in Leicester so he could send photographs home to his mother. This first date was a great success, and the couple have been together ever since. In fact, they hit it off so well on that first date that when the military authorities locked down the camp at Shady Lane in preparation for Operation Market-Garden William had a date arranged with Doreen that he would obviously need to break. He opted to do this in person which meant going AWOL (absent without leave) and shortly after he arrived at Doreen's house to break the bad news, the MPs rolled up to take him back!

Subsequently Sgt. Kline was wounded in or near Nijmegen in Holland on 28th September and was shipped back to America once he had recovered enough to do so. Doreen joined him some time later and he spent the next year in hospital recovering fully from his wounds.

Mixed tennis obviously had its attractions as this picture which was entitled "Tennis Cuties" clearly shows. It appeared in the book "Saga of the All American" (a history of the 82nd Airborne Division) which was first published in 1946.

The Clock Tower was a focal point in Leicester's town centre that proved to be a popular meeting place, and "meet you at the clock tower" was very often the arrangement for after hour's activities with the latest girlfriend, or perhaps a group of buddies. This landmark was only a relatively short double deck bus ride away for men of the 504. Also, being in the centre of town it wasn't far away from all the popular pubs and dancehalls. (The picture on the left was taken in 1942, so the clock tower appears just as it would have to the 504 paratroopers).

Pfc. Walter E. Hughes wrote of his time in England:

"Most of my memories of the camp at Leicester were pulling guard duty, training, and the rain. The country around the camp and Leicester was beautiful. I was born and grew up in Brooklyn NY a big part of NY City. On a practice training jump the surrounding country looked like one big patchwork quilt. But it did rain a lot. It looked like we would wear out the raincoats before anything else. For my part, the people of England were good to us. They had endured so much for so long and still remained determined and so very courageous.

I arrived at the camp in mid August when training was picking up for what everyone knew would be another combat jump for the Regiment. I was assigned to what I believe was the First Platoon, the Sgt's name was George Davis I think, there was also a little guy, Sgt Sam Cleckner, he was from Ohio. The tents we shared were in neat rows and each one held five troopers. In the middle was a stove. I was told that the camp was some sort of English Estate and any digging was prohibited so the latrines were all huge buckets that were periodically emptied by local farmers. There was no fence around the camp only a thick hedge. The only fence was the guardhouse fence if I remember rightly.

Pulling guard duty could be a wet affair

I didn't expect to be able to get into town because of the training, but after a week I did receive a pass and some of the guys said they would introduce me to a nice place to go dancing. Not being a dancer I was not interested, but headed for someplace to find a drink, which I did on most of my days on pass. I remember the "Swan with the two necks" and the "Royal Hotel" I think. The beer was strong and warm, but we got used to it. There was a tough old barman I remember who had fought in WWI. I believe his name was Harold or maybe Harry and when he bellowed out, "Time ladies and gents, and you too Yanks!" You got the message! One of the most hilarious incidents I remember from our time in

Walt Hughes (on left) today, with another former 504 trooper, Bill Leonard

Leicester occurred in one of the pubs. It involved a friend from Camden New Jersey, Cecil Curry, and another trooper called John Murphy. We had been drinking fairly steady and were, as we say feeling no pain. Cecil was almost legless but he said he was going to the latrine. As we were having a good time we forgot all about Cecil; that is until closing time when it was time to leave. Then we realized he was gone a long time. We went out to where the latrine was, in this case the back yard where there was a cement wall with a sort of narrow trough along the bottom which when people would urinate, would carry it into some sort of hole. Well poor Cecil had passed out and fell in that trough and had laid in there for at least an hour, with many G.I.'s doing there thing right on him as everything was blacked out so no one could see him. When we finally found him he was a sight, and smelled to high heaven. Now how were we to get him back to camp? We couldn't take a bus, the truck had already left, and by this time all three of us were just plain exhausted. We found a house with a small front yard and fell asleep behind some bushes. About 4:00am the sound of a jeep woke me up and it was from H Company. We conned the driver who had just left his girl friend to take us back to camp where we all headed for the showers because the jeep driver said we all smelled like we wet ourselves all night long.

On another occasion I had been on guard duty all night down in an area of the camp that some construction work was going on. I don't even remember what it was. After a couple hours' sleep I hitched a ride into town, and proceeded to drink in one of the pubs. What with not eating and being tired, it didn't take long for the strong English Beer (Stout or bitter) to get me feeling good. There were four US Air Force Sgt's sitting at a corner table that were also feeling no pain, and were obviously in a lousy mood. A couple of remarks were extended my way about my shinny boots and something else I didn't quite hear. I was alone and I thought the only Airborne Trooper there. I sized them up and figured I was in for it, but if I could get a couple of good shots at the bigger one first I might be able to scare the others, or at least make it easier to get out. Just as they started to make there moves I heard a booming voice from behind a petition," I say lads; I think the odds are a bit off-sided don't you. And three Brit' Red Devils came out and stood alongside me. The Air Force G.I.'s took one look and made for the door. I finished out the day with those three guys and we all got stupid drunk. I think of that incident and often wonder if any of those Troopers ever got out of Arnhem alive.

I had a hard time trying to figure out the exchange rate in the money and relied on the honesty of the people who I was buying anything from. Having just left the States and my girlfriend I was not as eager at first to become involved with any of the local girls as some of the old timers who had been in Italy. However, the English girls were so much like home that I eventually did meet a

very nice girl. We walked the streets of Leicester and went to a movie but it went nowhere, and before it could, the regiment departed for Holland.

I hope you like this of me! It was taken in October, or September, I cant quite remember! Ha, ha! that rhymes! R.

After the war ended and we were stationed near Salisbury, before heading home I made the acquaintance of a girl named Rosemary Yarrow. I still have her pictures in a photo album (right), of course with the permission of my dear wife of 53 years Mary. I often wonder about her, she became a singer with a band. I knew the name of it but can't remember it now. She had a beautiful voice. When she sang in the Red Cross Club, her mother was always with her. When I walked out with her, her mom was not far behind us. We corresponded for a few years after I came home, but in 1950 I met my wife and that ended the letters.

It transpires that Walt's young lady with a beautiful voice became renowned vocalist Rosemary Squires MBE! (Rosemary is still performing today, and was a great favourite of The Queen Mother). She well remembers Walter, or Eddie as she and her family new him:

"I well recall Walter E Hughes, who we knew as Eddie, as a tall, good looking American soldier with a very honest face. The war had ended and as an antidote to my rather dull day job in 'Kelly's Directories' my evenings were much more exciting singing with local bands. I think it must have been at the American Red Cross Club that Eddie asked to walk me home where he met my family who took to him immediately.

From time to time my family had offered homely hospitality to servicemen stationed nearby and Eddie came around a number of times for some of mother's egg and chips, which would be repaid with the famous American 'Hershey' candy bars! But it must have been but a matter of weeks before he was shipped back to the States.

We corresponded for a while when the family, especially my father, eagerly awaited his long and interesting descriptions of the places visited in his work for the Russell tugboat company. Everything American was especially glamorous to those of us who had not travelled far from our small town existence. As so often happens the letters dropped off. My career as a singer took off nationally and I

Rosemary Squires today – still singing

guess it was about that time that he met Mary, and having seen her photograph who can blame

Newlyweds Walt and Mary on the Russell Tugboat 20 in 1952

him! I still have some of his letters and snapshots even a badge of the 82nd Parachute Regiment, which he sent through the post. Though there was nothing romantic between us just an old-fashioned platonic short-term friendship.

My sister and I have often wondered how 'Eddie' had fared in life and little did we expect to renew contact almost sixty years later. It is good to know that he found happiness with Mary who he obviously adores. Deservedly so - Eddie was a perfect gentleman in every way."

Many of the paratroopers were invited for meals "at home" with local families, Cpl. David S. Stanford of I Company (from Perrysburg, Ohio) wrote home about just such an invite:

"Dear Friends,

Was glad to hear from you all once again and to know you are all in good health and spirits. Can say the same from this end, and long may it continue thusly. For once I have something to write about which I think would interest any woman, to cut a long story down to a minimum, will just say was invited to an English home for tea yesterday "Sunday". Having time on my hands I

accepted. Upon arrival at the fore mentioned home I was quite taken by the beauty of the place, a colossial (misspelled) old brick mansion, don't know exactly how old and didn't wish to embarrass myself or host by asking, but gathered from conversation that many an ancestor had dwelled there. The rear of the house is covered by those creeping Rose vines, and they are in full bloom, and the flower garden and lawn surpass any I have ever seen including those of our River Road homes. Inside the house it was cool and quiet, floors were of tiles, and small throw rugs of beautiful design were sprinkled about generously, was informed by my host, a very wealthy middle aged gent, and somewhat proudly I thought, that they were hand made by my hosts mother. Surprising thing was the modern-ness of the interior of the home, fireplaces were electrically controlled, and they have an air conditioning unit that accounts for the coolness. Then we had tea before we embarked on a cycle through the near countryside, by cycle I'm speaking of bicycle. The tea was a nicely done thing, and what really thrilled me was the fact that the silverware we used was once property of the Duke of Cambridge. Whoever he was, must have been a strong fellow, cause I swear the knives alone weighed a pound.

After tea and our ride of an hour or so in the afternoon air, we retired to listen to the late afternoon news, was the first time I had lofted in an easy chair for quite some time and you may be sure made the best of the opportunity, upon taking my leave was asked to return this coming Thursday evening, so will let you all know from time to time how am getting along, was afraid of my manners yesterday, but guess must have gotten by alright.

Guess have rambled on enough for this time so for now will close and get ready for "chow". Hope we have something good, as I'm hungry as a bear.

Hope to hear from you all again very soon,

Your friend,

David"

Cpl. Stanford was subsequently posted as MIA (Missing in Action) on 27th September 1944 around the Den Heuvel woods area in Holland, his body was never found.

Writing about his time in England, Lt James Megellas, H Company, recalled in his outstanding book "All the way to Berlin" (published March 2003 by Presidio Publishing):

The "Donut Dollies" of Clubmobile K

Photo Courtesy of www.clubmobile.org

"Among the many pleasantries we encountered in England was the Red Cross Clubmobile that served us coffee and doughnuts. Clubmobile K and the three lovely ladies who operated it – Mary, Charlotte, and Marianne; the "Doughnut Dollies" seemed to always be in the vicinity of the 504. We enjoyed not only the coffee and doughnuts, but on occasions, the pleasure of their company as well. Captain Carl Kapper, Rivers, and I escorted them to dances

and social functions, and occasionally on the rounds in Leicester." The picture shows from left to right: Charlotte Colburn, Mary Moore, and Marianne Shellabarger; Lt. Megellas's "Doughnut Dollies" of Clubmobile K. Charlotte wrote home of her first encounter with the men of the 504th:

"Yesterday we visited one of the parachute groups that have just come from Italy. We stayed for supper and afterwards drank beer with them – they are a crazy wild gang, taught us how to jump from a dummy plane. The entire gang of eight are escorting four of us to a dance tomorrow, and so it goes, the tough life in the ETO."

The girls were obviously very popular and their efforts received a mention in "The Panel" news sheet:

Photo Courtesy of www.clubmobile.org
An example of the American Red Cross Clubmobile
mentioned by Lt. Megellas

"THANKS GIRLS"

That was a pretty nice little doughnut party we had yesterday afternoon, what with the Artillery band sounding like something off the "bandwagon", and Alma and Charlotte making beautifully with the doughnuts. Thanks a lot. How about a date next week same time, same place!

Doreen Newson of Leicester was a pretty 15-year-old (left) when the 504 descended on Leicester. Although only quite young she was never the less pursued by eager young paratroopers. She recalls walking through town on one occasion with her mother and being asked out by a GI, who even offered to bring his buddy along for her sister (mother!). Eventually Doreen fell for a young paratrooper, Cpl. Lee Eastman of Hq and Hq Company (right). He promised to come back for her after the war, but was sadly killed in action on 7th April 1945 at Hitdorf am Rhein whilst crossing the river into Germany. Doreen, who is trying to research the circumstances of Lee's death, has recently travelled to America to meet his twin brother and family.

Cpl.Lee Eastman

Another local girls' story thankfully had a happier ending…..

Jean Harvey, an eighteen year old from Evington was swept off her feet by a dashing young trooper from the 504; James McIver from Service Company:

"I remember my friend setting me and Jim up on a blind date. We were both very shy and hardly said a word to each other all night. We started seeing each other more and more and realised we got on really well"

Then on 17th September Jim went on the Market Garden Operation to Holland with the rest of the regiment, but he never forgot Jean. She picks the story up again:

"It must have been about a year later and I was on my bicycle and had just picked some Bluebells to take home. I went home and there he was. He just asked me if I wanted to go to the jewellery shop".

They got engaged, and in 1946 Jean boarded the Queen Elizabeth 1 ocean liner bound for the U.S. to marry Jim.

Jim recalls his first impressions of Leicester:

"When we were over here, we thought Leicester was the greatest place in the world. We had travelled all over to all sorts of war torn places. My overriding memory when we arrived here (at the church) was seeing all these lovely big, clean, shiny windows, none of them was smashed".

Deryk Wills (President of the UK chapter of the C47 Club), Jim McIver, and the Author at the Shady Lane site.

I spent an interesting hour walking round the Shady Lane site with Jim (who had been with the 504 from North Africa, through Sicily, Italy, and on through Holland eventually to Germany and the end of the war in Europe), but sadly it has changed so much in the last 60 years that he couldn't really remember much of it although he had a good idea where the motor pool had been.

Jim commented rather ironically that the PoW's that came along after the 504 had left had a better time of it as at least they got wooden huts for accommodation, were as the paratroopers had to make do with tents! (Sadly in November 2006, a year after I met Jim he lost his battle against cancer and passed away).

We also visited the local church, St. Denys in Evington (which is situated very close to where the unit was encamped), where a Stars and Stripes flag hangs in one corner. Captain Delbert A. Kuehl (left), the regiments Anglican Chaplin had struck up a friendship with the local clergy at St. Denys, which resulted in the Americans being welcomed into the church for their Sunday services, and the flags presentation to the people of Evington by the Regiment in a special service on 13th August 1944 by the regiments CO, Col. Ruben Tucker.

There is also a commemorative certificate, which tells of a generous donation (£200 – nearly $1000 back then) made by the Officers and men of the 504 prior to the Regiment leaving Leicestershire for Holland on 17th September. The money was used to build an extension, which included the vestry on the side of the church.

ST. DENY'S CHURCH, EVINGTON, LEICESTER   M 5096

I showed Jim the photo below of the 504 parading through Oadby, suggesting that he would have been involved. He grinned (and winked) and said it was unlikely as he usually managed to find someone of sufficiently high rank who desperately needed a ride in a Jeep on such occasions!

The picture above (courtesy of Deryk Wills) shows the 504 marching through Oadby (London Road) during the "Salute the Soldier" parade in May 1944. This event was run right across the country as a fund-raising exercise, Leicester's target was £3.5 million, and the eventual figure the city raised was reportedly £3,541,757. Oadby was given a target of £100,000, quite a sum for what was a small village at the time. For anyone familiar with Oadby, next to the timber-framed building (which has since been demolished) to the left of the Stars and Stripes flag is Ragg's the Butchers, and Swatland's Off-licence can just be seen on the extreme left of the photograph. The two houses in the immediate background are due to be knocked down shortly to make way for a new development. The photo below is virtually the same photograph taken in March 2006.

Behind the photographer would be the Black Dog Pub and the Fox Inn (below and left), either

side of the Albion Street junction, and just across the road from St. Peter's Church and the War memorial. Both establishments were frequented by men of the 504 as well as other units of the 82nd. (Incidentally, the Fox Inn is where I bought my first pint of beer, it cost me 11 new pence way back in nineteen hundred and seventy something!)

An 82nd 'trooper, although not a 504 guy (Richard Halberstadt – a T5 corporal with 782nd Airborne Ordinance Company) is pictured here outside the door of the

Black Dog Pub in August 1944, he must have been pretty hot in those "Class A's" (best uniform – mostly wool) in August!

The Black Dog Pub, Oadby

Richard met a local girl, Elizabeth Tower at an Oadby church hall dance, she had been cold-shouldering most of the Americans as they couldn't dance 'properly', but Richard was an excellent dance partner, and Elizabeth eventually thawed. They got engaged in September 1944, and the couple were married after the war (August 1946) at St. Peters Church, Oadby. Richard took his new bride

Elizabeth and Richard Halberstadt

back to America, were they have been happily married ever since.

Left is St. Peter's Church, Oadby, a small number of 82nd Airborne 'Troopers were married here after the war.

As mentioned above, through a friendship struck up between Captain Delbert A. Kuehl the 504's Anglican Chaplin and the local clergy the Regiment gained the use of the nearby church, St.

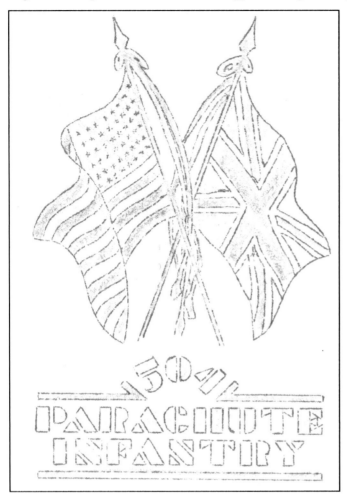

Deny's. They held regular Sunday services there, which are well remembered by local lad John Collier, who attended them with his family. Amazingly, John saved some of the church service sheets and has provided copies, some of which are reproduced here.

The copy (facing sheet opposite) below dated 13th August 1944 includes the presentation of the regiments Stars and Stripes battle flag to the people of Evington by the Commanding Officer, Colonel Rueben Tucker, and a solo (The Crucifixion) sung by Miss Louise Shepherd.

The Evening Mail newspaper covered the presentation in its edition on the 14th August:

AMERICANS GIVE BATTLE FLAG TO A LEICESTERSHIRE CHURCH

A unique ceremony took place at a church in Leicestershire yesterday, when

SUNDAY AUGUST 13, 1944   1000 HOURS
Service Sponsor . Hq Co , 1st Bn.
Company Commander . Capt Anderson
Ushers . Pfc Harry Roberts
Pvt Harry Dunaway

Prelude

Doxology . . . Page 5

Invocation

Hymn . Praise Him , Praise Him . 91

Offeratory . . Announcements

Word of Greeting by the Lord Mayor
. Mr. Gillot

Presentation of the American Flag
by Colonel Reuben K. Tucker
504th Parachute Infantry
Solo . The Crucifixion
sung by Miss Louise Shepherd

Morning Prayer

Message . "Great Men of Faith"
Captain Kuehl

Hymn . I Would Be True . 108

Benediction

Postlude
Organist . Cpl John W Link

One recollection of combat which will forever remain imbedded in our minds is the self evidence of the statement made by a Chaplain in the Philippines - "There Are No Atheists in Foxholes. Many times have we all called on God to provide the necessary driving force and staying power which have gallantly maintained the Regimental Motto - 'STRIKE and HOLD'.......

There is no doubt of our determination as Parachute Troops to always do our utmost for our Country . Let us at all times and places leave as little doubt of our determination to do our utmost in the Service of the Lord

H. R. Williams Jr

Lt Colonel , 504th Prcht Inf

at a special US Army parade service, the commanding officer of an American unit presented the vicar of the church with the regiments battle flag. The flag, which led the Americans on three great campaigns – the African, Sicilian and Italian – will in future hang in the church.

The commanding officer explained to the large congregation of American soldiers and villagers the significance of the gesture.

"We are" he said, "presenting a small token of our appreciation of the way in which all of you have received us into your community. We shall all be eternally grateful, and I wasn't to present this flag to be kept here in the church. It is not a new flag, but one that has flown in front of the regiment since the beginning, through Africa, Sicily and Italy, and means a great deal more to us than a new flag would mean".

The vicar of the church said: "You have this morning done us in this parish a very great honour in presenting to us the flag of your regiment, which is new in one way. It has created history that, in years to come, will be talked about throughout the world".

"This flag will hang in the church, we trust, for many generations, perhaps centuries, as some of the flags have in our cathedrals".

"It will serve to remind coming generations of the sacrifices we in this generation have made, and as people will gaze upon the Stars and Stripes they will renew themselves in a fresh dedication of the English speaking peoples to cement that friendship and understanding, which we trust, will be a guarantee to world peace for many years, if not for all time."

The copy on this page is significant as it is date Sunday 4th June 1944, two days prior to D-Day, Operation Overlord, and the Invasion of mainland Europe from Normandy on Tuesday 6th June 1944. It is sobering to think that two of the regiment's men who volunteered for D-Day duties and were KIA on the 6th (although obviously they didn't know it) only had 48 hours or so left to live.

Once the regiment had left England to take part in the Market Garden Operations in Holland the 504's chaplain, Captain

Study to shew thyself approved unto God, a workman that needeth not to be ashamed . . . . II Timothy 2:15

Sunday June 4, 1944 1000 hours

Prelude

Doxology . . Page 5

Invocation

Hymn - All Hail The Power of Jesus Name - 60
Offeratory - Announcements

Hymn - Amazing Grace - 78

Morning Prayer

Special Music - "He Lifted Me"
Sung by Cpl Alex Lester
Message - "A Patriot for Christ"

Hymn - When The Roll Is Called Up Yonder - Page 3
Benediction

Postlude
Organist - Pfc John W. Link

The grace of the Lord Jesus Christ, and the love of God, and the communion of the Holy Spirit, be with you all . . II Cod. 13:14

NIEMOELER'S LAST SERMON

Martin Niemoeller - submarine commander in the last war - decorated for bravery - became a minister - now in prison. . . . . .

"There is indeed no hope," said this German pastor who will not worship Hitler, "except to hold firmly to the Crucified One and to learn to say in simple and certain faith, 'In the bottom of my heart Thy name and cross alone shine forth at all times and in all hours, and therefore I can be glad.' It may be long until we are truly glad, until like the apostles we are counted worthy to suffer shame for Jesus name. The way will not be opened today or tomorrow. And that may be good, for it may teach us not to take impressions for belief. It may teach us how, in the heat of the struggle, to mark the word of the Lord and continue to hear the message of the cross, the Gospel of Jesus Christ - perhaps for the first time aright. It may show us how to teach it and to hear it and to preach it, for our faith lives in this word, and our joy flows from this word. 'Lord, evermore give us this bread.'" . . . .

Delbert Kuehl wrote to the Reverend Richardson, vicar of St. Deny's at the time, expressing his gratitude towards the people of Evington:

```
          OFFICE OF THE CHAPLAIN
          504th Parachute Infantry
          APO 469          U S Army
            Delbert A. Kuehl




                                   26ᵗʰ September 1944



     Reverend Richardson
     Vicar
     Evington Parish Church


     Dear Reverend Richardson and Members of Evington Parish
     Church:

          It is with sincere gratitude that I extend on the
     behalf of the Commanding Officer, the officers and men
     of the 504th Parachute Infantry our thanks for your kind
     reception of our unit into your community and Church.
     We have learned to know many of you and do cherish that
     friendship. We do pray that many of us have shown the
     high qualities that we desire to see in our fighting men,
     and that you will forgive those who have left any stain
     on their uniform and the America they represent.

          We in uniform have had a pleasant example in this
     community of the English people and their beautiful
     country side, and I can say with the deepest meaning
     both have been wonderful. Formerly we have had contact
     with your fighting men on the battlefield - now we are
     beside them again. Their determination in battle is no
     doubt a direct result of their great heritage. We will
     work and fight together, so that when we meet again we
     may stand under the Union Jack and Stars and Stripes
     floating over lands blessed with peace.


          In the Service of our Country and our Lord,



                         Delbert Kuehl

                         Delbert Kuehl
                         Chaplain
                         504th Parachute Infantry
```

In his memoirs, "Casablanca to VE Day, Darrell G. Harris of Hq & Hq Company describes what he remembers of his stay in Leicestershire (and English social habits of the time):

"When we arrived in England, one of the first things we noticed was how green the countryside looked after the brown winter hills of Italy. The next thing we noticed (or this could have been the first) was that the girls spoke English. Maybe they spoke with a different accent and a strange pronunciation of some words, but it was English never the less. We bivouacked near Leicester (pronounced Lester), a three penny coin was called a thrupny bit, and bus fare was two and a half pence (tuppence haypenny). Pubs (short for public house) had names like The Hare and Hounds, the Haunch of Venison, and The Crown and Thistle. Beer was served warm, but we quickly adapted to that, and we learned how to order a "pint of bitter" or a "half and half" (pronounced awf and awf). Any hard liquor was called spirits, and it was rationed by limiting the number of bottles sold during each opening. Little old ladies would bring flasks in their purses, order a tot of spirits (most seemed to prefer Gin), drink half and pour half into their flasks, and order another until the quota for that day was gone. Pubs were open only during certain hours, and at closing time the bartender would call, "Time, gentlemen, please," or "Now gents, towel is on", which had to do with the practice of throwing a bar towel over the spigots to signify that no more beer could be served.

A 504 'trooper (Lloyd Gates, I Co. from Altoona PA) enjoys (!) a pint of warm British beer – always good to the last drop!!

Pubs were more than just places to go drinking; they were neighbourhood social centres. Many had pram rows where mothers would park their perambulators, complete with babies, while they socialized with each other, and with other patrons. They all new which pram belonged to whom and would call out if any baby needed attention. Remember there was no television at the time to keep people occupied at home. Sometimes there would be sing-a-longs with songs such as "The White Cliffs of Dover", Lili Marlene" (borrowed from the enemy), and bawdy tunes like "Roll me Over in the Clover (Roll Me Over lay me down and do it again).

Double Decker buses and taxicabs which could make U-turns in a narrow two lane streets, were other things that impressed us. Some of the Brits had seen a few American movies, and when they learned I was from Texas they started calling me Tex. Everything was rationed in England during the war, Movie houses in Leicester were still operating, but there was no fuel for heating, so it was wise to wear a coat to the movies and leave it on. They made their own jokes about English weather such as "We have nice summers here in England. Last year it fell on the fourteenth of July." They were on their wartime equivalent of daylight savings time, called Double British Summertime, and it would still be daylight until after 10 p.m.

We had not been paid for sometime before our arrival in England. Payroll was held up for some reason, but Colonel Tucker made arrangements with some of the local banks to cash cheques for us. The exchange rate at the time was almost exactly four dollars per pound, so currency conversion was easy. Twenty shillings to the pound and twelve pence to the shilling required a little more calculation, but we quickly adjusted to that too.

So we spent the summer in England. Got some leave time to places like Morecombe and Blackpool, and I even got to spend a couple of days in London. I suffered appendicitis and had my appendix removed in England. Just my luck it happened then, so I didn't miss any combat.

We engaged in manoeuvres and made a couple of practice jumps, but we sat out the Normandy Invasion. A few of the guys went as pathfinders. I halfway expected to be selected for that mission as I had been to Pathfinder school at Pomigliano, but I guess they had all they needed before the got down to me".

Sgt. Albert Tarbell of H Company, a Native American Red Indian of the Mohawk tribe became friendly with a local family named Pell from Oadby and was asked, and proudly agreed to be their new daughter Sandra's Godfather. This was shortly before the Market Garden Operation in September. Once the regiment left on that operation they didn't return to these shores, and sadly Albert lost touch with his Goddaughter. However, he never forgot her, and eventually enlisted the help of the local newspaper, The Leicester Mercury to try and find her. The cutting shown here appeared in the paper in 1993, and shortly afterwards with a little help from local historian Deryk Wills Sandra made contact with her long lost Godfather.

His long lost god daughter

A veteran of the United States 82nd Airborne Division wants help in finding friends he knew 49 years ago.

Albert Tarbell of the 504 Parachute Infantry Regiment, which was camped in Shady Lane, Evington, is trying to find his god-daughter.

It seems that he got to know a family by the name of **Pell** while he was here. All he can remember is that the mother's name was **Eileen**, the father was in the RAF and the brother-in-law was in the British Airborne. He thinks the family lived in Oadby.

Albert, from New York, was asked to be god-father to **Sandra** at her christening in 1944. If Sandra reads this, perhaps she will get in touch.

The 504 left Leicester in the September to parachute into Holland for the Market Garden Operation. They fought their way across Europe never to return to England.

Sgt. Tarbell returned to America late in 1945 after completing occupation duties in Berlin, and returned to civilian life. He subsequently had 5 children of his own, and his son Mike eventually followed in his father's footsteps and became a paratrooper with the 101st Airborne, serving three tours on active duty in Vietnam! Father and son have recently, along with others, become the subject of a book "Brave Men, Gentle Heroes: American fathers and sons in World War 2 and Vietnam" written by Michael Takiff. (Published by William Morrow October 2003).

Photos: Above right is Albert's son Mike in Vietnam. Opposite are Albert and Mike today.

Below is Albert's first letter to his Goddaughter for nearly 50 years:

"Dear Sandra,

Just think! We are corresponding after 49 years! I have thought of you and your mother throughout these years. All I did was look at your baby picture and the picture of your mother in the Air Force uniform.

I survived the jump in Holland. I was also on that first wave on the Waal River crossing for the bridge at Nijmegen. After that I went though all of the Bulge fighting and through to Northern Germany to Ludwiglust, Germany. I ended up for 6 months after the war with my Colonel in Berlin.

My daughter Karen was walking and talking. She was 2 months old when I left for Africa and Italy.

I went to work doing Ironwork in Construction. My wife Cecelia and I had five more children through the years. I retired in 1985 from construction work. My wife Cecelia and I did extensive travelling, until she took sick and passed away in June of 1988.

I remarried in April of 1991. Dorothy is her name. She is a wonderful person.

This is a rather quick letter I am writing. We have just come back from Nashville, Tennessee for my airborne reunion.

I am very sorry to hear Eileen is ill. I have the fondest memories of her. Please give her a big hug and kiss for me.

I will write about the children in my next letter, if you would like to hear from me again. I have told my children that I received word of your whereabouts, they all new of my Goddaughter in Leicester.

I will be celebrating my 70th birthday this Tuesday, the 24th of August. Please write and tell me about your life. We have a lot of catching up to do. Please send a photo of your mother and yourself.

Dorothy and I are looking forward to hearing from you,

Love

Albert."

Albert and other members of H Company formed up on the golf course at Evington.
The picture was taken shortly after the regiments' arrival from Italy in late April 1944.

From Michael Takiff's book "Brave Men, Gentle Heroes" (Published by William Morrow – Oct. 2003) Sgt. Tarbell recalls:

"Right after D-Day a few of us rode our bikes up a long hill – there was an English pub there that we went to. We were sitting having this warm beer and there was a bunch of locals. They kept looking at us, eyeing us. Finally one of them says, "How come you guys are here enjoying yourself? We got all these people there in France. They're sleeping on the cold ground, and they're not getting no beer. They're not enjoying themselves."

I told him, "Look, we saw action in Italy, and now we're trying to get enough men to go back into combat." I say's, "Do you know this man sitting over here?" And I pointed to Rosy – his name was David Rosenkrantz; everyone just called him "Rosy". And Rosy's face started getting all red. That's the kind of guy he was – he started to blush.

I said, "He's a hero."

The guy says, "What do you mean?"
"He captured two hundred Italian prisoners". When he was in Sicily - before I joined the outfit – he got captured by the Italians. He ended up coming back to camp two weeks later with two hundred prisoners – they all surrendered to him. We used to laugh about that.

My God, once I told them about Rosy, we couldn't drink enough beer. They were giving their rations of liquor to us. We left there, and we had to go down that steep hill on our bicycles. I don't know how we made that sharp turn."

Sgt. Rosenkrantz's heroics were reported in The Los Angeles Daily News thus:

200 Italians Dine Their 2 Captors

WITH THE AMERICAN TROOPS IN SICILY, July 15 -- (UP) When Sgt. David Rosenkrantz of Los Angeles and Cpl Lee Black of Jackson, Tenn., United States paratroopers, landed outside the town of Scicli they ran smack into 200 Italians.

The Italians held a conference and decided they were the ones who ought to surrender. Rosenkrantz and Black agreed to turn them over at the first opportunity and then everyone sat down to dinner with the mayor of the town providing plenty of wine.

As soon as Yank reinforcements appeared after daylight, the Italian colonel formed his command and headed by Rosenkrantz and Black marched to their surrender--singing.

Source: Los Angeles Daily News, July 16, 1943

On August 11ᵗʰ 1944 the 504 along with the rest of the 82ⁿᵈ Airborne Division had a very important visitor, General Eisenhower. He reviewed the 504 and the rest of the Division at RAF Leicester East Airfield (Stoughton Aerodrome). Apparently the weather was very warm, and the tarmac turned into sticky, tarry glue for about two hundred yards along the front of the generals' reviewing stand, making marching in step and with any sense of pride and élan almost impossible. Ike took it all in good spirits and when the "march past" was over and the division assembled in front of him to hear his words, the men all stood on their helmets in order to see. The officers took a pretty dim view of this, but Ike spoke up saying words to the effect "these guys deserve a chance to see the man who is sending them into battle! Let them stand on their helmets if they wish!" He gained a lot of respect from the men with that, it was the typical "IKE" they all loved.

Lt. James Megellas recalled Ike's review of the division in his book "All the Way to Berlin":

"Off places and events with the 504ᵗʰ, parades seldom left a lasting impression on me, but I never forgot the division review for Ike, not because of the parade itself but for the remarks he made to the troops from the reviewing stand. Most of what he said I would categorize as boilerplate from a commander to the troops, except for a brief remark. This is almost verbatim: "You men have accomplished great things and I have greater things in store for you."

Down the ranks of paratroopers standing in formation, 10,000 Adam's apples went up and down in unison. "Greater things in store for you" had a different meaning for us than it did for him. For us it meant that after the next "Greater things", one half to three fourths of us standing in the ranks would not be returning. That was our experience from the invasion of Anzio, and there was no reason to believe that an invasion somewhere else in Europe would be any different."

Brenda Keyworth (below) was an 18 year old telephone operator who worked at the Oadby Telephone Exchange. The regiment had two telephone lines directly from the camp at Shady Lane to the exchange, and Brenda used to talk to several of the paratroopers during the quiet times. One Sunday she was on duty until 2 pm, and she got talking to Wilmer Keith Hart who was 25 and ran communications for Hq Company. He asked to meet her, and once she had finished work she rode her bicycle out to Shady Lane:

"I rode my bike to Shady Lane, where he (Keith) was waiting for me on the bridge, Pants creased and boots shinning, he seemed a nice fellow. He walked me all the way home (I lived on the Glen Road at the time) where he met my family. I told him I was going on holiday the next day, but I don't think he believed me; he thought I was giving him the brush-off, so he turned up at the telephone exchange the next day and ended up taking another girl out!

Being the persistent type (and one would expect nothing less from a 504 paratrooper), *a week later Keith tried again, and I met him under the chestnut tree at the top of the village near the Sandhust Street School (pictured below) - this then became our regular meeting place. From that point I saw him several times a week. One day I got home to find him washing the dishes, "my mother" he said, "had gone to town" (meaning the village, Oadby) - I mistakenly wondered why she had to go to Leicester?*

Keith Hart

We would ride to Wigston for fish and chip's, and to Leicester for the movies. We also used to ride out to the Tea Pot café which was on the Harborough Road on the way to Great Glen for very English pots of tea. He always treated me with the greatest of respect, and eventually asked me to marry him. We got engaged on August 2nd, and despite the rationing my parents managed to get a bottle of wine and some food together. A Christmas wedding was planned, but of course didn't come to pass as Keith along with the rest of the regiment jumped into Holland that September.

We wrote many letters, I think I wrote over three hundred, I used to number them so he would know if any were missing. Just over a year later on September 20th 1945 Keith returned to England, and we hurried to get a wedding together. This took place at the Charles Street Baptist Church in Leicester on September 24th.

The previous Saturday we had been walking down the London Road in Leicester across from the railway station just as a 504 'trooper (Jim Bryant) came out of the station. Keith yelled across the street "Hi Jim, what are you doing Monday", to which the answer was "Nothing" – "Well, how about being my best man"; and so it was!

We honeymooned in Blackpool, and after Keith's furlough finished he went back to Germany, and was eventually shipped back home to the USA on December 3rd 1945. I followed a few months later in April 1946 on the Queen Mary, and then a long train journey to Denver, where we made our home for many years. We had four son's, all born in the US, and now have ten grandchildren, and 6 great grandchildren. Sadly Keith passed away in October 1992 from a severe stroke. He was buried at Fort Logan, Littleton, Colerado.

Keith and Brenda Hart on their Wedding day, 24th September 1945

Pfc. David Finney of HQ & HQ Company recalls settling in at Shady Lane and a planned weekend in nearby Nottingham that ended with a bang on the head! (During his stay in the UK

David spent a 72 hour pass sight seeing in Edinburgh with some friends and the portrait shown below was taken at that time)

"It took about a week before we could really say we had settled in. A roof over our heads, so to speak, cots to sleep on and food was served three times a day. As we would say back home in Tennessee, we were living "High on the hog" (sumptuous living). What a restful place. Then we were back into regular army life. Roll calls, callisthenics, marches and all the other military stuff. Not much fun but necessary. Another plus was being able to take showers whenever we wanted to or had time for. Little things like this would have been luxuries before we left Italy.

I became acquainted with Leicester by checking out the city. I never cared for (warm British) beer but it seemed to be the "thing" to do. I never acquired the taste and began going to the movies at the Odeon Cinema (I think that was the name of the place). I was able to meet females at the pubs so would order my beer just to fit in. Then I met this great looking ATS girl. We hit it off in no time flat. We both had plans for the following day so we would meet the following weekend. The week went by slowly until the next Friday night. We met at the designated place (I don't remember where. Not important.) We caught a train to Nottingham for the fleeting weekend. We made plans for the following weekend if we had time off.

We met at the train station. One thing was different; she had brought her best friend from her company. The three of us boarded the train for Nottingham. We made our way to this pub we had been at last week. The owner of the place supplied us with Scotch whiskey. This pleased us. I think we drank until we could feel no pain. We just had too much. We were leaving the pub for our hotel. As we left someone yelled with the remark that "Yanks are overpaid and get all the birds." I really didn't know what the expression 'birds' meant. We continued outside without looking back. Suddenly something hit me on the head, I fell to the pavement. My next remembrance was a cop (Bobby) shaking me. As I opened my eyes I could see a crowd around us. A police officer, an ambulance and medical attendants were over me. The officer asked if I wanted to file charges against the soldier that had hit me from behind. Not wanting to cause him any trouble I said "no." They put me into the ambulance and my two girl friends rode along to the hospital. I spent the night. The next morning I was released around 10 AM. The attendant informed me that due to the alcohol consumption plus being very fatigued played a roll in my black out when I was hit in the head. This is what we called a "sucker punch." My ATS friend had spent the night with me at the hospital. Her friend had gone back to Leicester. In all..............what a LOST WEEK-END! Anyway, we made our way back to Leicester and remained friends, nothing serious. We both realized that we were living for today and tomorrow would take care of itself. After several weeks resting here in England, we suddenly slipped out to Spanhoe Airfield for Operation Market Garden.

I can't say that all of the English people were nice to us, but, on the other hand, many G.I's were rude, obnoxious and insulting to our host........England and the many kind, thoughtful and wonderful people of your country".

Pvt. Edwin M. Clements of B Company remembers arriving in England as a replacement with little else but the rank of Corporal (most of his kit would appear to have been lost in transit – something modern day airlines still seem to be good at doing!). Even the two stripes were to cause some problems, and his Company Commander in true Paratrooper fashion soon provided a solution!

Photo Courtesy of
www.bcompany504pir.org

"We docked in Liverpool in the dead of night. It was raining and foggy and it took us over two hours to unload, collect our two huge duffel bags and get on the trucks that would take us to our assigned units. Except that my two bags could not be found, and the trucks couldn't wait. Even though the bags were heavily labelled and marked with my name, rank, and serial number I never saw them again including the beautiful monogrammed Dopp kit and a number of other personal items that my parents had thoughtfully sent with me. So off I go to win the war with a small musette bag containing shaving stuff, a bunch of dirty underwear, and a few pair of socks. We unloaded while it was still dark. I was told to find a cot in a 12-man tent. All I knew was that I was in the 82nd Airborne Division and we were in a camp near the city of Leicester--pronounced 'Lester'. It was pitch dark and I was cursed loudly since I woke two men by stepping on them. Finally I found an empty cot and without undressing--except for my boots--fell on the cot and slept. In the morning I awoke to the usual sound of reveille and found that I was now a part of the First Platoon, B Company, 1st Battalion, of the 504 Parachute Infantry Regiment, which had seen action in North Africa, Sicily, and most recently Italy, including a long and hazardous period on the Anzio beachhead.

I quickly found that my squad leader was a young man whose name was Jerry Murphy. Murphy put me in touch with the Company Supply Sergeant, one of the more memorable characters in B Company. The role of the supply man was to keep the company supplied with everything they needed on and off the line. Sgt. Hyde heard my sad story and very quickly supplied me with almost everything I needed in terms of clothing and equipment. But the true measure of Hyde's efficiency was his ability to beg, borrow, scrounge, and even steal if necessary when the usual sources of supply had dried up. I remember a period in Holland when rations were very short because the road over which re-supply took place periodically was cut by German units. Hyde disappeared for about ten hours. Early the next morning he pulled up in front of what constituted Company Headquarters in an open Jeep. The entire front and back seats were filled to overflowing in cooked pork chops! He not only provided us with a memorable meal, he presented the Company Commander with the Jeep.

Murphy, although acting as Squad Leader, was still a Private though he was in a job which called for Sergeant's stripes. I had come over with the two stripes of a Corporal on my sleeve, which apparently created a bit of a problem. Later that day it was resolved when I was told to report to the Company Commander, Captain Helgeson. He could have served as a perfect role model for a WWII parachute officer. Not tall, but wide-shouldered, thin-wasted, and flat-bellied, he was also blonde and blue-eyed. His uniform was spotless, his boots glistened and he came to the point quickly. "Corporal Clements, your rank and training entitle you to fill the job of an assistant squad leader of a rifle squad even though you have never been in combat. I am sure you would not feel comfortable leading a squad of combat veterans who have been in combat in Sicily, Salerno, and on the Anzio beachhead." He didn't wait for my response. "Therefore, I am demoting you to 'Private' immediately - You are dismissed!"

Pvt. Edwin Bayley was a late replacement that arrived in England after the 504 had left for Holland and Operation Market Garden on 17th September:

"In the early evening of a day in late September or about the first week of October a bunch of us replacements from the USA arrived in England on board the British Ship Mauretania. We billeted at a replacement depot near Liverpool and then were posted to the 82nd Airborne Parachute School at Ashwell near Leicester. After we had been assigned living quarters and fed, our barracks group of twenty men discovered during chatting and getting acquainted that eighteen of us had supposedly been in some type of confinement ranging from city jails, state jails and penitentiaries!

The first evening we were shown the mess hall and the recreation room, where the eternal crap game was continually played. Some of the airborne cadre looked a bit old for jump duty but they were still very physically fit for training purposes. One grizzled old sergeant had on a jump suit with five pound noted falling from almost every pocket.

Training at Ashwell started each morning with long stretches of double time running, push-ups and other strenuous physical training, rope climbing, and tests for mental alertness. Afternoons were devoted to instruction and practice on handling parachutes, using harnesses suspended from the training building roof. We were awed by the ability of the instructors to do several hundred push-ups on one hand. Some instructors made rope climbing with one hand look easy. We practiced exiting the plane through a mock door. After a week of this we were taken to a nearby airport for our first of a series of five

Jump School at Ashwell, a stick of trainees prepare to make a jump.

53

jumps. We did not have practice towers, as did the students back in the USA. All of our jumps were from planes. Our landing field was a small one near the Ashwell barracks and tents. Anyone who refused to jump was sent to the 325th Glider Infantry Regiment.

We had some interesting times. We were confined to the camp area at night but some of the students managed to sneak out and visit a local pub. One of our men accidentally broke a beer glass one night. He was told that (because of rationing) replacement glasses were hard to come by. He compensated by entertaining the pub crowd by eating the broken glass fragments!

The landing field had several high straw or haystacks up to about 20 ft. tall. One of our troopers decided to land on one of these only to land up to his hips in cow manure, as this was a stack of it covered by straw. He had to be hosed down before being let back into his tent. There were stronger than desired winds on our final jump day but we had to jump and get out of Ashwell before the next class arrived. My final jump landed me in a turnip patch with the tops of the turnips about 2 inches above ground level. I was dragged on my stomach for about a 100 ft. before I could collapse the chute. After the fifth jump we received our wings and jump boots.

A few days later we boarded trucks and went to the 504 Camp at Evington, (probably about mid-October). There was a line of 4 to 6 man tents along a camp roadway leading straight down from the main gate. After being assigned to tents we were shown the mess hall, the recreation room and the evening Red Cross doughnut line. The camp sanitary facilities were very primitive, an outdoor latrine with a canvas wall across the back and sides and big buckets below wood seats for toilets (possibly Eddie Livingston's Honey Pots). The American soldier stockade prisoners had the detail of emptying and cleaning these each day.

When our group arrived at the Evington camp the rest of the regiment was in Holland having jumped into a successful Market Garden operation. While we were in Evington we went through minor training exercises including night marches and compass training in brush land. While we were there the camp life was quite relaxed, without much to do. Passes were issued for evenings and daytime Saturdays and Sundays for the Leicester area. The men went to the pubs for a beer, to the movies and just out with the girls of which there seemed to be an inexhaustible supply. They were everywhere. After a few weeks we were told to get our gear ready for transfer to some place.

We boarded C47 transports and in a couple hours or so found ourselves in a small isolated landing strip area (no buildings) in Central France. We were trucked several miles to an empty French army barracks near Sissonne. The barracks consisted of many large concrete constructed two and three story buildings, several large one-story mess halls and lots of small warehouses and garages. Our mission was to prepare the barracks for the arrival of the 504 from the Netherlands. It was now late October and very cold at night. We had stoves for which we went to local wooded areas to cut wood for fuel. The green wood did not always burn very well so the troopers would help the fire along with a bit of petrol. Some of the stovepipes were hooked up to chimneys and others to the barracks ventilating system ducts. One day in our barracks section someone threw in a bit more than the usual amount of petrol on a delayed ignition. The vapours got into the vent system and when ignition finally occurred there was a loud explosion, accompanied by falling ceilings! When the 504 arrived at Sissonne from Holland, I was assigned to the first platoon, Company A, the group I stayed with until leaving Berlin the following August (1945).

54

Chapter 3.

A Normandy Excursion.
(504 Paratroopers volunteer for Overlord).

Pathfinder
Insignia

Although this book is primarily concerned with the time the 504 spent in England, I believe it is only right and proper to briefly look at the 504's involvement with the D Day operations, as the events occurred during that time frame.

It was assumed at the time that the 504 would be joining the rest of the 82nd Airborne for the forthcoming invasion of Hitler's "Fortress Europe" in Normandy. As D-Day approached however, it became clear that the 504 would be held back. The regiment had after all been through a pretty tough time in Italy, and a lack of replacements for its losses it would seem prevented it from participating in the invasion, (although General Gavin had seen the unit after it got to England and commented that it appeared to be in fine spirit and good shape) so it was to be held back in reserve. In the end however, a couple of dozen or so 504 troopers were picked from about 50 volunteers who trained as Pathfinders to take part in the D-Day operations, and dropped into Normandy on the night of the 5th/6th June. They were to be deployed as security details for the Pathfinder units (and no doubt a steadying hand of experience) with the in-experienced and combat green 507 and 508 Parachute Infantry Regiments.

Listed below are the details of the volunteers who took part:

Name	Number	Company	Pathfinder Stick/Unit	Comments	State
Lt. GOETHE James	0425992	A Coy	3/507	Deceased 1991	SC
Lt. MURPHY Thomas	01313430	HQ/3	2/508	POW Dec. 1987	PA
ADERTON Curry	17044260	HQ/2	2/507	Deceased June 1984	MT
BALDASSAR John	33366649	H Coy	3/508	KIA 28.09.1944	PA
BYRNE Joseph	32801540	H Coy	508	KIA 17.06.1944	NY
CATON Arthur Jnr.	35473067	HQ/2	3/507	Deceased 1991	KY
CHANEY Walter	13072994	F Coy	2/507	Deceased 1995	MD
CUNDIFF Amos	6991728	A Coy	1/508	Deceased 13/06/1972	MA
DICKINSON John	38020882	HQ/1	507	POW Dec.1977	OK
ENDSLEY Edward	6297375	B Coy	2/507	Deceased July 1983	OK
EVANICK Michael	32000715	F Coy	2/507	POW Dec. Sept.'85	NY
FORKAPA Nick	15329875	I Coy	2/508	Deceased 1965	OH

GRAY William	14030502	B Coy	3/507	KIA 06/06/1944	NC
HANNIGAN William	20751497	H Coy	1/508		NE
LIVINGSTON Eddie	14001361	I Coy	2/508	POW Dec.22/03/2002	AL
MANFREDI Joseph	32769867	E Coy	508	KIA 14/06/1944	NJ
MCCARTHY Thomas	11047965	A Coy	3/507	Deceased 11/11/2002	MA
MORTZFELDT John	16065045	A Coy	1/507	Deceased 21/03/2001	MI
MURDOCK Hal	14065678	I Coy	3/508	POW Dec.19/05/1957	GA
PARCHMAN Cicero	38202422	G Coy	3/508	POW Dec. 4/06/1996	CA
PAWLINGS Henry	32745415	G Coy	3/508	KIA 06/06/1944	NY
RIGOPOULOS John	11105947	H Coy	3/508	KIA 20/09/1944	MA
RODGERS Thomas	20421704	C Coy	3/507	KIA 15/06/1944	AL
SHIPTON Bernard	12055219	B Coy	2/507	Deceased 02/03/1989	NY
TERNOSKY John	33463601	I Coy	2/508	Deceased 10/05/1995	PA

As mentioned elsewhere, four other members of the 504 jumped on the 5th/6th June. Two officers, Lt. Thomas Graham and Captain Willard Harrison were picked for their experience and toughness in combat. The 504's XO, Lt. Colonel Charles Billingsea went as an observer, and an enlisted man named Donald Crooks. All four jumped with General Gavin as part of a 508 stick, and landed in a 507 drop zone. Donald Crooks, an enlisted man was recommended to Gavin by Col. Tucker as "the toughest man in the Regiment" and was to serve as Gavin's bodyguard. He later received a battlefield commission. (The picture left is of Lt. Donald Crooks in Belgium; Donald survived the war but eventually lost his battle against cancer and passed away on 5th June 2001). General Gavin remembered Crooks in his book "On to Berlin":

"Another man was given to me by Colonel Tucker of the 504th Parachute Infantry; Colonel Tucker insisted that I allow him to come along, saying he was the toughest soldier he had in the regiment – and that was saying an awful lot. This man wore a gold earring in one ear and didn't do much talking, but he had a reputation for being a very rough character indeed. The tragedy is that I never saw him from the moment we went out the door. I suspect he was worried about me and went looking for me and was killed."

Plane (chalk) 18 – 508 PIR. Third row (standing) 3rd trooper from the right is Pvt. Cicero Parchman, second row (kneeling) 2nd from left is Pvt. Henry Pawlings, 3rd from left is Pvt. John Baldassar, and 4th from left is Pvt. John Rigopoulos. Hal Murdock also jumped with this stick, and is possibly 5th from left (standing), but I haven't made a positive identification as yet.

Plane (chalk) 17 – 508 PIR. In the aircraft door is 2nd Lt. Thomas Murphy, 3rd row (standing) far right is Pvt. Nick Forkapa standing next to his good friend Pvt. Eddie Livingston. John Ternosky is probably on this photograph, but I have not been able to identify him so far.

Plane (Chalk) 16 – 508 PIR. Amos Cundiff, William Hannigan, and possibly Joseph Byrne and Joseph Manfredi jumped with this stick, but as yet I haven't managed to identify them.

Plane (Chalk) 15 – 507PIR. Pfc. John Mortzfeldt is on the front row, 3rd from the left; Arthur Caton, John Dickenson, and Walter Chaney are also amongst this stick of 507 Pathfinders. (Fred Baldino was a good friend of John Mortzfeldts' and he told me that John had said that if he ever got back to America he would go up into the mountains to live, where nobody could find him. Apparently he was true to his word and went into the mountains in Michigan, where he lived with his dogs until he died in 2001).

Plane (Chalk) 14 – 507 PIR. Pvt. Bernard Shipton is standing 4th from the left, Pvt. Edward Endsley is standing 2nd from right. Pvt's. Curry Adderton and Michael Evanick, are also in this photo, but I have not been able to identify them (possibly standing left in aircraft door, and standing 5th from right although I'm not sure which one is which).

Plane (Chalk) 13 – 507 PIR. Lt. James Goethe is far left kneeling, Thomas L. Rodgers is 3rd from left standing, William Gray is 5th left standing, and Thomas McCarthy is 4th right standing.

Pfc Bonnie Roberts again recalls:

"When they invaded Normandy, we hadn't been back too long so we weren't ready for it. So they left us behind. A friend of mine named Jose Sandoval went in with them to Normandy as a pathfinder. I was real happy that I wasn't to go. As I might have not been here if I did go in."

(Strangely Jose Sandoval is not listed as having been one of the 504 troopers that jumped, but I guess over 60 years one's memory can plays tricks, either that or my sources are incorrect! - it has also been suggested that certain other members of the 504 did in fact take part in the operation, although not on pathfinder duties).

Fred Baldino was also happy that he didn't have to go to Normandy:

"Because we were under strength from all the action in Italy, we did not jump into France on 6 June 1944 - D-Day - but there were about twenty-seven men from the 504th Regiment who had volunteered to go in as pathfinder".

When those that volunteered for, and survived Normandy (five were KIA, five were taken as Prisoners of War, and approximately half of the remainder were wounded) returned to England, there was a two-week period of debriefing to endure. They were then let loose in Leicester for some fun and relaxation before the retraining of the regiments' replacements began. Some of the men were suffering from scabies caught in Italy, and were not too keen to report the "irritation" to the medical staff for fear of being confined to camp; it is reported that many Leicester girls suffered the same fate sooner or later. Some say that the situation became so acute that 'troopers who had been cured were being re-infected by locals that had originally fallen victim to the 'troopers themselves. Apparently those free from the curse spent a long time eyeing up a potential partner (to see if they were scratching covertly) prior to introducing themselves!

All those who volunteered for duty in Normandy received the Bronze Star for their efforts.

Pfc. Thomas L. Rodgers was amongst those KIA, and he was posthumously awarded the Distinguished Service Cross for his actions. His citation read:

"Private First Class THOMAS L. RODGERS, 20421704, Infantry United States Army for extraordinary heroism in connection with military operations against an enemy of the United States. Having jumped into NORMANDY in the vicinity of AMFREVILLE FRANCE on June 6, 1944, Private First Class RODGERS, observing many of his comrades pinned down by enemy machine gun and small arms fire, moved without hesitation to destroy the enemy. Mounting a stonewall, in full view of the enemy, he neutralized the machine gun position and proceeded forward, driving back the enemy with effective fire from his Browning automatic rifle. During this action Private First Class RODGERS killed or wounded 25 of the enemy and made possible the organization and advance of our troops in the area. His personal courage, aggressive leadership and courageous inspiration contributed materially to the success of his comrades and typified the highest traditions of the service. Private First Class RODGERS was later killed in action against the enemy. Entered military service from Alabama."

The DSC

T.L. Rodgers was one of a small group of friends that Ross Carter wrote about in his book "Those Devils in Baggy Pants", he was affectionately known as "Big Rodgers", his volunteering for Normandy was covered thus:

"T.L. Rodgers and twenty-four more of our boys volunteered for detached duty in Normandy. We gravely shook hands with the giant, a gnawing anxiety chewing into our gizzards. Big Rodgers was more than just a member of the platoon. He was a staunch pillar in our ranks both morally and physically. He radiated a quiet encouragement that sustained our confidence. In battle he manifested a courage that translated itself into deeds and a bulwark of security for us all. When on outpost or patrol duty with him, I always had the feeling that things were well in hand.
"Be careful, T.L." I said.
He hesitated as was his custom before answering: "I'll be as careful as I can, Ross, but I may not be careful enough this time." Then he left us. That evening we drank several bottles of ale and toasted Big Rodgers on every bottle."

Major Willard Harrison, one of the officers who jumped with General Gavin was also awarded the Distinguished Service Cross, his citation reads as follows:

Major Willard E. Harrison, 0395975. 504th Parachute Infantry, United States Army, for extraordinary heroism in action against the enemy on 9 June 1944 in France. When the company commander of a tank company was killed in action at the bridge over the Merderet River, Major Harrison, realizing there was no officer in that company who was sufficiently cognizant of the immediate plan of action, immediately went forward. Though subjected to heavy rifle, machine gun, mortar, and artillery fire, Major Harrison personally carried orders to each tank commander in the company. Without regard for his own safety, Major Harrison fearlessly moved the tanks on foot, directed them to their proper positions in the assault force and stayed with them until their mission was accomplished. The personal bravery, initiative and superior leadership displayed by Major Harrison reflects great credit on himself and is in keeping with the highest traditions of the Armed Forces. Entered military service from Nebraska.

Pvt. Eddie Livingston's Form DA1577 reflects that he was awarded the Distinguished Service Cross as well, but for some unknown reason he was never actually presented with it (subsequent research through several archives by 82nd pathfinder expert Mr. Dave Berry has also failed to locate any reference to a citation). He got the award for the action he was involved in that culminated in his capture as a Prisoner of War on the 9th June 1944. Eddie wrote about the action in some detail in his narrative "The First Time I saw Paris":

"I made it 'til 9 June '44, after many hair-raising encounters with the Germans. My previous combat experience made the difference. About mid-afternoon on the 9th June I was moving warily through the countryside; striking any enemy in my path and disappearing. I figured I had it made! When sounds of firing reached me, I could hear some M1's and burp guns. There was much more enemy fire than friendly, the friendly fire was ragged, not steady, often with just a single M1 firing. I stopped for a breath and to think. From the sound of the firing, I could tell the Germans were pressing some jokers hard! Knowing full well that I was making a mistake, perhaps a fatal one, I headed for the sound of firing.
I came upon a road junction, near-by-to St. Mere Eglies. The road junction was a very important position strategically. There were 15 to 20 jokers at the road junction, sheltering behind a hedgerow and low stone wall. One or two of the jokers were duelling with the Germans across a small open field. The Germans had taken shelter in a small wood, a goose-neck-like protrusion into the field. Both sides were firing across the open field.

All but one of the jokers were wounded, most seriously, one died a minute or two after I arrived. I had field glasses, and I could see what appeared to be a platoon of Germans in the wooded protrusion, and they were trying to set up a mortar. The low stone wall afforded ample shelter from rifle and machinegun fire, but I knew that if the Germans got the mortar set up, they could angle the shells over the wall, lobbing then flush on top of the jokers, and it would be "Katy-goodbye!", jokers and position would be lost. A little voice in one ear kept saying, "get lost Livingston! You volunteered for this son-of-a-bitch, and it has blew all to hell now! Your job is done! Get lost! Use your god-dam head joker!" the little voice urged, "Stay here and you are dead, dead, DEAD!"

I would be a liar if I said I wasn't tempted to just turn and get lost. I knew god-dam well that I could take care of myself, for a month if need be, and hurt the enemy plenty in the process.

One of the jokers, MG Marsh, 82nd Division HQ, seemed to be in charge, he was the only unwounded joker. Marsh had jumped with the 508th, but not with P.F.T. He had also been with the 504th through most of its combat, he was a Cpl. He had been a jump-school instructor, and had been jumpmaster for me on my first three school jumps. Marsh told me an officer, a glider pilot, had been with them at the road junction, but had gone away to round up more jokers, leaving Marsh in charge, telling him to hold the strategic position at all costs till he returned with reinforcements.

"It's a hopeless proposition," I told Marsh, "unless we can knock out that mortar quickly!" Marsh and one or two of the less seriously wounded had been duelling with the Germans across the open field, but now the Germans were ominously quiet. I kept my glasses on the one setting up the mortar. In combat, experience is a great teacher. I knew that the mortar had to be knocked out, quickly! Greatly surprised I found I had already abandoned the idea of turning tail, taking off, and getting lost! "Well, god-dam-it! I hadn't come to France to dance!" and I was a lousy dancer any old way!

I carefully estimated the distance from the stone wall to grenade range of that mortar. It was approximately 150 yards of open unobstructed field, and the wheat had been trampled flat; a good run. But I was fast, very fast, and a shifty runner!

I said I was fast, with the proper incentive, I could fly, but I needed to know the type of weapons, aside from the mortar and the usual burp guns and rifles I would be facing, also the calibre of the soldiers themselves.

I deliberately exposed myself. Hopped over the wall and capered out towards the wooded protrusion. Marsh thought I had gone crazy, but the Germans took the bait. Their fire was erratic and high. There was a short burst from a machine-gun, less steady and higher than the rifles and burp guns. The erratic and high fire indicated to me that the enemy troops were probably green, or nervous, maybe both. The machinegun fire being unsteady and high indicated some important things; one: It was probably not properly emplaced; two: the crew was probably not familiar with it, maybe both. I also learnt the type gun it was. From hard necessity I had learned the combat capabilities of the German, and his weapons.

Even though I had found out many things about the enemy across the way, I was still not satisfied with my intelligence. Too much was at stake – My life! I deliberately exposed myself again. Between exposures I had stripped myself of all but bare essentials. Two grenades, pins pulled, one double clip (two clips taped together) for the Thompson. Discarding helmet, excess ammo. Etc. On my second exposure the enemy fire was even more erratic, and the machinegun didn't fire at all. And I had danced way out, offering a really inviting target before scampering back over the wall. I figured I had a good chance to get in close enough to use those two grenades on that mortar before the Germans could recover and bring their fire down to a dangerous level. I gave my glasses, name etc., to Marsh and asked him to notify my outfit if anything happened.

I topped the wall running! Bent low, flying actually, a shifty zigzag course! But the Germans had outsmarted me, they had recognised my deliberate exposures for the information seeking subterfuges they were. Their fire came down quickly, steady! Swing wide them Pearly gates, Fire up that Fiery furnace! Cursing myself for a god-dam idiot, I was forced to hit the ground far short of grenade range. I hit the ground rolling and scrambling forward. That machinegun had opened up again with a vengeance. I had to get in under that machinegun fire quickly, or die! That krauthead son-of-a-bitch had fooled me plenty! He could play that baby like Sugar Ray punching the light bag.

I kept scrambling forward, with the slugs and those little red devil German concussion grenades eating up the ground around me! After what seemed an eternity and a half, I was close enough for my grenades, I let them fly, readied my Thompson, and only just in time. The Germans, except for the ones at the mortar came at me in a rush. Out of about 15 to 20, just four reached me, I got the rest with my Thompson.

The mortar went up in a thunderous blast as my grenades landed smack on target. I am not certain, but I think that smart son-of-a-bitch on the machinegun fled.

By then the four remaining Germans and I were whirling on the ground in a desperate hand- to-hand struggle. The outcome was inevitable, I was already winded from running and scrambling, they smothered me with shear weight of numbers. Those Germans were big and blonde, I was 5' 6", and. 155lbs, I did get to my knee's once, only to be flattened by a burp gun smash that all but peeled my nose from my face. My Thompson had been snatched from me. The Germans then proceeded to kick and beat me senseless. I kept trying to get my jump-knife in the sheath on my boot. But it just wasn't my day!

Marsh, helpless to intervene, watched the action from behind the wall with my glasses. Later, after the Germans carried me away, the officer glider pilot w/o Kirby returned with reinforcements, and the jokers and position were saved."

It would appear that although (several weeks later back in England) Marsh related the incident to Eddies CO, Capt. Moffat Burriss of "I" Company, his platoon sergeant, S/Sgt. William H White (left), and also First Sergeant Odom (right), and suggested that the action was worth at least the DSC, and they all agreed, the action was eventually forgotten. Eddie was however awarded the Bronze Star with Combat V for valour. Eddies' full story can be found on the Internet at www.eddiesplace.org. It seems that Eddie had a pretty tough time of things when he eventually got home, and the website is dedicated to his memory and is an attempt to help other veterans who find themselves in similar boots.

A few weeks after the incident, in October 1944 Eddies mother wrote to his Commanding Officer enquiring as to the whereabouts of her son, she received this letter in response from Capt. Burriss:

COMPANY "I" 504TH PARACHUTE INFANTRY
APO 469   U S ARMY

October 16, 1944

My Dear Mrs. Livingston,

        I received your letter of October 1, 1944, asking for
further information concerning your son Pvt. Eddie Livingston,
who has been missing in action since June 6, 1944.
        Pvt. Livingston was a member of a volunteer group of men
who were the first to land in France on the "Invasion" on
June 6, 1944. He and the others were to prepare the way for
the Paratroopers who came in later. They flew to France by
plane, and some of the men who were in his plane saw him jump
with the others, and land by parachute. When the group assembled
later on the ground, he was not among them.
        For his heroic action in being one of the first to "Invade
the Continent", he was awarded the Bronze Star. I will see that
the Medal is sent to you as soon as possible.
        I, also, was very sorry to hear, Eddie was missing, because
he was an excellent soldier while he was in my Company. He always
tried to do what was right, and never complained, regardless of
the hardships.
        In the future, if I receive any more information concerning
the where abouts of your son, I will write to you and let you
know immediately. I sincerely hope that he is found, for he
was well liked by all the men and his Officers, and was an excell
ent soldier.

                              Thomas M. Burriss

                              THOMAS M. BURRISS
                              Capt., 504th Prcht Inf.,
                                Commanding "I" Co.

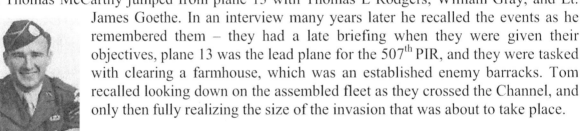

Sgt. Thomas McCarthy jumped from plane 13 with Thomas L Rodgers, William Gray, and Lt. James Goethe. In an interview many years later he recalled the events as he remembered them – they had a late briefing when they were given their objectives, plane 13 was the lead plane for the 507th PIR, and they were tasked with clearing a farmhouse, which was an established enemy barracks. Tom recalled looking down on the assembled fleet as they crossed the Channel, and only then fully realizing the size of the invasion that was about to take place.

Once over the drop zone, with a full moon, it was almost like jumping in daylight and he could see the Germans on the ground firing up at them as they floated down under their canopies. He had a very close shave on the way down when a German bullet creased his left temple, and remembers being "madder 'n hell" that he was bleeding before he'd even reached the ground! He landed near a well by a large farmhouse, and recall that T.L. Rodgers landed in the courtyard of the farm buildings – he could hear him engage the Germans with his B.A.R (Browning Automatic Rifle) – "after a while it went quiet and I thought that the Germans had got Rodgers", he said (this was not the case as Rodgers survived until the 15th when he was KIA). He hid in some long grass whilst two Germans searched for him, and when the opportunity arose, tossed a hand-grenade at them, killing them both.

After a while, he began to search for other paratroopers from his group and then became aware of a steadily increasing drone overhead, looking up he could see large numbers of parachutes floating earthwards – the main drops had begun. He recalled his first contact with a friendly 'trooper, who he felt was "greener 'n hell" and was lying in a hedgerow, he snuck up on the guy, all the time worrying that he'd get shot by one of his own side – eventually the 'trooper challenged him and they exchanged passwords, Tom told him he'd been dam lucky because "If I'd been a kraut, you'd have been dead"!

66

Tom and his newfound partner eventually became casualties of a mortar round that landed close to them. He was blown to the ground, and knocked out for a short while. When he came too, he realized he'd taken several small pieces of shrapnel in his back, and that Kates (the other 'trooper) had been quite badly hit in the leg. They eventually made it to an aid station where Tom again passed out through loss of blood.

Sgt. McCathy survived the war, and eventually passed away in November 2002.

A memorial service was held for the men of the Division who were killed in Normandy.

In the mean time the rest of the Regiment stayed in England training, and "dry runs" came one after another. Several missions were scheduled for France, Belgium, and Holland, but all were cancelled at the last moment for one reason or another – on one occasion the troopers waited for three days for fog to lift so that they could drop into Belgium only to find when the weather had cleared sufficiently that General Patton's Army had overrun the drop zone, and their services were therefore not required.

I have been able to track down a number of photographs of some of the 504 Officers and enlisted men who took part in the D-day operations.

Pfc William L. Gray
KIA 6 June 1944

Pfc. John Mortzfeldt

Pvt. Eddie H. Livingston
PoW 9 June 1944

Pfc. Bernard G. Shipton

Sgt. Thomas McCarthy

Pfc John Rigopoulos
KIA 20 Sept. 1944

Pfc. John Baldassar
KIA 28 Sept.1944

Pfc. Thomas L. Rodgers
KIA 15 June 1944

Pvt. Cicero Parchman

Pvt. Henry Pawlings
KIA 6 june 44

Pvt. Edward Endsley

Pvt. Nick Forkapa

Lt. Thomas Murphy

Lt. James Goethe

Lt. Col. Charles Billingslea

Lt. Donald Crooks

Chapter 4.

All Good Things Must Eventually End.
(The 504 PIR leave Leicestershire and England).

England, like Naples before, was beginning to become a little mundane for the men of the 504. It was certainly better than Italy or North Africa had been, almost like being back home in lots of ways. The local population had been very welcoming, warm and friendly, but the daily grind of training, inspections, and reviews, practice jumps, and the usual activities that accompany garrison life made each day seem more monotonous than the last. The veteran paratrooper's, who had been battered and bruised in previous campaigns in Sicily and Italy, knew better than to hope for another combat mission, but they wanted to go somewhere, anywhere to get away from the monotony of garrison life.

Then on September 15th word came, and the word was that a mission was proposed to jump ahead of General Dempsey's British Second Army. The men had by this time become so used to false alarms that they didn't take "the word" too seriously, and the subsequent briefing seemed to confirm their scepticism. The operation called for the Airborne Army to drop into Holland, and secure several bridges over the numerous waterways that were so much a part of the central and southern Dutch countryside. This would then give the British Tanks a clear path to the Zuyder Zee, and provide the Allies with a left flank sweep around the Germans Siegfried Line defences. If it came off, it would be a jump that would do much to end the war quickly (by Christmas some said).

Members of H Company prior to embarking for Market Garden

Nobody believed that this operation would be carried out; the 504 were to jump with other units of the 82nd Airborne Division, landing fifty seven miles behind enemy lines in the vicinity of Grave, Holland, to capture the longest span bridge in Europe over the Maas River, along with two other bridges over the Maas-Waal Canal.

When the details of the plan became clear, E Company was to jump south of the Maas River. The remainder of the 2nd Battalion would descend north of the river, and between them form a grip on the Grave Bridge that Supreme Headquarters had ordered to be taken at all costs. The 1st Battalion was to jump farther north and take bridges Seven and Eight over the Maas-Waal Canal; the 3rd Battalion would jump between the 1st and 2nd Battalions, and for the initial part of the mission, be in reserve.

To the men of the 504, this plan seemed to be even more incredible than a couple of jumps that had been proposed for Rome and Capua whilst they had been in Italy - especially when they were told that the line of flight would be over the Scheldt Estuary; a route that Allied bomber pilots had appropriately named "flak alley".

It seemed even more incredible when it was revealed that there were supposedly 4,000 SS troops and a German tank park in the area, the battle-wise paratroopers laughed up their sleeves; this had to be a "dry run", because tanks were definitely bad news for airborne troops, and in addition to this, the enemy would have overwhelming superiority in numbers.

However, as time went by no word of cancellation was received, and the morning of the 16th dawned with a typically heavy British fog hanging over the airfield, even if command was serious about this operation, it would be impossible to take off in these conditions. As if to make things worse, a light rain began to fall and the paratroopers were expecting at any minute to be told to return to their camp. That afternoon, however, invasion currency was issued and word was received that tomorrow, the 17th, they would be going regardless of the weather.

The following are exerts from a report written by Captain Karl Kappel of H Company on the days and hours leading up to the start of the operation and are typical of the whole regiments experiences:

"3rd Battalion, 504, with other units, was sealed in Spanhoe Airbase, 21:30 hrs 15th September 1944. Canvas cots and blankets were provided in the hangars by the Air Force. Battalion field kitchens were set up by the airborne agencies.

Early next morning, 16 September, unit briefings were conducted, each man was issued a 1:50,000 map of Groesbeek and vicinity, a 1:200,000 map of the Netherlands, a partial pay in Netherlands, Belgium, and German currency, and a gammon grenade with plastic explosives (As soon as the grenades were fashioned [shaped?] they were collected and kept in platoon piles), and two K rations and one D ration were drawn. The basic load of ammunition had been issued prior to arrival at the departure base. The remainder of the morning was free for the men to write letters, visit the Red Cross mobile units, and check personal equipment. The afternoon was spent loading and checking bundle release mechanisms, and loading and tying bundles.

Motion pictures for entertainment were held in the evening concurrently with pilot – jumpmaster conferences, C.O. meetings, and rehashing of each plan of action. The regiment at this time was probably at the peak of its fighting efficiency. For the first time since the invasion of Sicily it was able to have an extended period of time off for rest and relaxation in congenial surroundings and an opportunity to train and fit replacements into the organisation prior to combat.

Sunday morning, 17 September, religious services were held for all denominations, after an exceptionally good meal. All members of the regiment were assembled to receive a pep talk from Colonel R H Tucker, regimental commander, ending with; "We must and will take the bridge" (Bridge 11 at Grave)."

The following memories of the hours leading up to the 17th September come from Pvt. Edwin M. Clemens:

"The veterans, who knew exactly what we were getting into, quietly went about their business, checking their equipment and writing that oft-delayed note to Mom and Dad or the girl friend. But a few were still making a lot of noise abetted by the bad whiskey smuggled into camp. It was late and raining hard when I finally turned in, and I could not sleep. I think I had finally dozed off when a very distinctive explosion woke me. I knew at once, or rather I guessed right, that it was a Gammon grenade accident. We heard later that one of the troopers was making up a Gammon grenade to

Members of I Company on 17th September 1944

carry on the airplane, which was strictly forbidden. No one knew what had happened, but two men were dead and others were wounded.

It was Sunday, September 17, 1944, and I woke from an uneasy sleep feeling queasy. Breakfast was out of the question, but I did gulp down a large GI coffee and a piece of bread. Roll was called and we were marched to the truck-loading area where we would be carried to the airfield, which we were told was on the outskirts of Nottingham. The airfield was filled with C-47's, but I didn't see any gliders. As soon as the pilot saw us he came over and introduced himself as "Jack Smith." He had red hair and a big smile. "Don't worry, I'm the best pilot in the Troop Carrier Command, and I'm going to hit your drop zone right on the button." I liked that. We all liked that. Most C-47 pilots hated carrying jumpers on a combat mission, for a very good reason. Somebody would be shooting at them all the way; when they neared the drop zone they would be flying low and slow, and they didn't have self-sealing gasoline tanks".

Ross Carters recalled in his book "Those Devils in Baggy Pants":

"As we sat in our tents at the airport, we recalled the pleasant days at Camp Stoughton (Shady Lane) *and particularly the poignancy of farewell kisses and embraces. We took it for granted that many of us would never return.*

The usual days of strained waiting finally shrivelled into hours. It was ten o'clock. The eight of us lay on our cots, sometimes going several minutes without speaking but thinking the same thought: Tomorrow night at this hour some of us will be dead. Who will it be?"

(Ross Carter was subsequently wounded but survived the war. Sadly he died from skin cancer in 1947).

Walter Hughes wrote of the days running up to the 17th September:

"Some of the veterans were busy trying to get papers filled out to get married and change their beneficiaries on insurance policies, I spent a lot of time writing home to my mother, brothers and a girl I knew, Betty Gratton. It was not serious but she was a good friend. And who knows about after the War. Then the orders were given through the chain of command, draw ammunition K-rations reels of wire, anything you might need for at least 3-4 days. I had packed and re-packed everything at least 3 or 4 times. We had been to the jump field several times, only to be disappointed and sent back to camp. But on Sept 15 it was back to the fields and the C-47's and on a rainy morning of the 17th the order was go. The sun came out as England became history to the men of the Division".

Pfc. Willard M. Strunk of A Company welcomed the operation as he was getting bored of garrison duties, but he was not too enthusiastic about making a day-light drop:

"We were told on September 15, but did not leave until September 17. It was getting awful boring sitting around in one spot, so any change was welcome. Training every day and garrison life was getting awful monotonous.

Pfc. Willard Strunk, A Company at Shady Lane. (Courtesy Frank van Lunteren),

The first reaction to a daylight jump was – the Germans would have us as sitting targets and to hold that many bridges and take

them during daylight hours is going to be tough. I don't think we had thoughts of ending the war by winter, but that it was going to be a long hard battle and edging closer to Berlin."

It was drizzling again when the paratroopers awoke on the following morning. By 09:00 however,

Douglas C-47 (Dakota's) lined up on an airfield somewhere in England in preparation for the start of the airborne part of Market Garden.

the skies were clearing, and the early autumn sun was trying hard to put in an appearance. A combination breakfast-dinner brunch, (or perhaps a condemned man's last meal as some would say!) of hot cakes and syrup, fried chicken with all the trimmings, and good hot coffee with apple pie, was given to the men of the 504 before plane loading began; if they survived long enough, their next meal would be in Holland.

Men of the 504 jumping into Holland at a Drop Zone near Grave.

The monument at the Grave Drop Zone today

The Monument at the road bridge over the river Mass at Grave (below), this was the first objective of the 504, and was taken shortly after they landed. The dedication reads:

"JOHN S. THOMPSON-BRUG".
Grave, 17 September 1944

E-Company, divided across eleven C-47 Skytrains, had been given the mission to take the south side of the Mass Bridge at Grave.

As a result of jumping to early, most of E company landed in the village Velp and its surrounding vicinity. In the lead aircraft Lt. Thompson saw, while standing in the open doorway of his C-47 that they were flying over the built-up area of Velp and decided to wait. Once above open ground, the remaining paratroopers jumped and landed in the Marspolder area closer to their objective: The Mass Bridge at Grave. Completely cut off from the rest of their unit, the decision was made to start the mission.

After heavy fighting, the south side of the bridge was taken. The mission completed successfully without sustaining any losses. Once the north side had also been taken, Colonel Tucker was informed that: "Bridge No. 11 is ours". With 15 men, Lt Thompson achieved what had been assigned to a whole company.

The Name "John S. Thompsom-Brug"

Was unveiled by his wife Mrs. Phyllis Thompson

Grave, 17 September 2004

As a matter of interest the regiments only Congressional Medal of Honour (which is the United States highest award for bravery) awarded during the Second World War was won by Pvt. John R Towle in Holland on 21st September 1944. It was posthumously awarded and the citation read as follows:

Rank and organization: Private, U.S. Army, Company C, 504th Parachute Infantry, 82d Airborne Division. Place and date: Near Oosterhout, Holland, 21 September 1944. Entered service at: Cleveland, Ohio. Birth: Cleveland, Ohio. G.O. No.: 18, 15 March 1945. Citation. For conspicuous gallantry and intrepidity at the risk of life above and beyond the call of duty on 21 September 1944, near Oosterhout, Holland. The rifle company in which Pvt. Towle served as rocket launcher gunner was occupying a defensive position in the west sector of the recently established Nijmegen bridgehead when a strong enemy force of approximately 100 infantry supported by 2 tanks and a half-track formed for a counterattack. With full knowledge of the disastrous consequences resulting not only to his company but to the entire bridgehead by an enemy breakthrough, Pvt. Towle immediately and without orders left his foxhole and moved 200 yards in the face of intense small-arms fire to a position on an exposed dike roadbed. From this precarious position Pvt. Towle fired his rocket launcher at and hit both tanks to his immediate front. Armoured skirting on both tanks prevented penetration by the projectiles, but both vehicles withdrew slightly damaged. Still under intense fire and fully exposed to the enemy, Pvt. Towle then engaged a nearby house which 9 Germans had entered and were using as a strongpoint and with 1 round killed all 9. Hurriedly replenishing his supply of ammunition, Pvt. Towle, motivated only by his high conception of duty which called for the destruction of the enemy at any cost, then rushed approximately 125 yards through grazing enemy fire to an exposed position from which he could engage the enemy half-track with his rocket launcher. While in a kneeling position preparatory to firing on the enemy vehicle, Pvt. Towle was mortally wounded by a mortar shell. By his heroic tenacity, at the price of his life, Pvt. Towle saved the lives of many of his comrades and was directly instrumental in breaking up the enemy counterattack.

Two of the 'troopers who volunteered for the D-Day operations were subsequently killed in Action whilst in Holland. John Rigapoulos' death is recorded in Lt. James Megellas's excellent book "All the way to Berlin", he quotes from a letter from Sgt. Tarbell of H Company, who was writing about events after the Waal crossing on 20th September: *"As I was making my way up to the dike road, I met Pfc. Rigapoulos. He showed me his left thumb, which had been shot off. He said, "Well, here's another Purple Heart". John Rigapoulos and I came from Jump School together, and joined as replacements in Anzio, Italy. He was also one of the volunteers for the Pathfinders in Normandy. He was killed shortly afterwards that afternoon".*

John was actually killed by sniper fire just after the river crossing as the 504 moved on Fort Lent.
Also from Lt. Megellas's book, it would appear that Rigapoulos's friend John Baldassar was killed in fighting around the Den Heuvel Woods just over a week later on the 28th September.

Both men are buried at the American Cemetery at Margraten in the Netherlands.

Margraten Cemetry and Monument.

Epilogue.

Normandy – June 2005 and Beyond.

June 2005.

As mentioned at the beginning of this book, sixty one years on from June '44 I was in Normandy for the first time, and taking part in a couple of re-enactments to remember and honour some of the men who made the ultimate sacrifice and put their lives on the line for the freedom we enjoy today.

The march back into Carantan.

The first event was a commemorative march, which started in Carantan and wound it's way around the Normandy countryside for about 15 kilometres taking in a number of historic and interesting sites, amongst them "Dead Mans Corner", and "Purple Heart Lane" to name but a couple. About 200 plus re-enactors of all nationalities completed the march. At the end, we all marched back into Carantan in good order to the applause of many of the local town's folk who had turned out to watch. We formed up in four (large) platoons and were addressed by the organisers prior to being dismissed and offered a well-deserved bottle of Coke!

The second re-enactment exercise we did was aptly called "Operation Night Drop". This was organised by our host for the week, Steve Lee. There were about 24 people involved, divided into four sections.

The exercise was to simulate a drop into unknown territory with a march to a pre-designated "RV", or possibly an advance to contact. Either way, it involved dropping each team off at an unknown location to simulate being dropped away from the planned Drop Zone, with the task of getting back to a central

The team after the Carantan Commemorative March.

point, which was to be the church at Ste-Marie-du-Mont in the time allotted, and as covertly as possible. All teams were dropped at different locations between H-hour, which was mid-night, and H-hour plus 30mins, with an on-target time at the "RV" of 05:00hrs. The distance to be covered by each team was approximately 15 kilometres. No team was to enter the village before 04:45hrs.

MEDIC! – a "Team 4" trooper gets some attention for blisters prior to the start of the Operation.

Each team was supposed to supply its own navigational aids, i.e. a map and compass, but I know of at least one team that didn't, and no, it wasn't our team!! In any event, all teams made it back to the "RV" on time, and I believe most, if not all enjoyed the experience and had a good time.

Personally, I know it served to give me a little idea as to what it must have been like to drop into an

Operation Night-Drop Team 4

unknown (and hostile) location that I hadn't been briefed on (as happened to a large percentage of the 82nd and 101st Airborne) in the dead of night. Then having to orientate oneself and advance to a known point of contact, all the time being mindful of the clock and enemy actions. Although there wasn't a real enemy to consider, and nobody was shooting at us we did spent a lot of time diving into road-side ditches and over walls and hedges to avoid detection by the not inconsiderable number of French motorists that were about at that time, and also "tactically withdrawing" (running away!!) from a large number of local dogs that seemed to reside at most farmhouses that we passed along the way, all of which barked loud enough to wake the dead, never mind their owners and other close residents!! (I guess if you considered each dog that we disturbed as an enemy guard, then there is a good chance that none of us would have made it to the "RV" alive - quite a sobering thought really!).

The Guys (Team Ditch-Diver 2005):

Cpl.Manny Trainor

Pvt. Pete Burden

Sgt. Steve Lee

Pvt. Jean-Marie Caillant

The Author

Sgt. Preston Wilson

Whilst in Normandy, I also took time out to visit the American Cemetery at Colleville-Sur-Mer, (which is at the top of Omaha Beach) to pay my respects to three of the five guys (William Gray, Henry Pawlings, and Joseph Byrne) from the 504 who jumped as pathfinders on the night of the 5th/6th June and paid the ultimate price (John Rigopoulos and John Baldassar were subsequently killed in action in Holland, during Operation Market Garden). I have to say it was a very moving occasion, but one that I would not have missed, and indeed felt was very necessary as no tribute to the 504th and the men who served in it would be complete without it. The cemetery itself is absolutely immaculately kept (as one would expect), and there is a great feeling of peace and tranquillity to be found there. Strangely, I also found the same feeling whilst visiting the beaches at Utah and Omaha.

Of the four others that are marked on the list as "killed in action", two appear in the records as being buried in the American Cemetery at Margraten in the Netherlands (John Baldassar, and John Rigopoulos), Thomas L Rodgers was transported back to America and is buried next to his father (who was a 1st World War veteran) at the Carolina Cemetery in Andalusia, Alabama. (Rodgers was posthumously awarded the Distinguished Service Cross for his actions in Normandy, his citation can be found elsewhere in this book), and I can find no record of the final resting place for Joseph Manfredi (as with Rodgers, his family may well have asked for him to be transported home for burial). Also the American War Graves web site does stress that there were nearly half a million American servicemen killed in WWII, and that they only have records of the final resting place for about 180,000, so I guess this is not uncommon (indeed there were a lot of grave stones at Colleville-Sur-Mer marked "known only to God").

The American War Cemetery at Colleville – Sur - Mer

June 2006.

Utah Beach: 06:00 hrs on Tuesday 6th June 2006 (after another Nightdrop exercise) – Being on the beach at that time was a very moving experience indeed.

October 2006.

On Sunday 1st of October 2006, a special service was held at St. Denys church, Evington, and a new

Stars and Stripes flag was presented to the congregation on behalf of the 504 Parachute Infantry Regiment by Deryk Wills (life member of the 82nd Airborne Division Association). This was to symbolise the continued ties between the regiment and the parish of St. Denys, and show that the regiment has not forgotten the goodwill and friendship shown to them by the people of Evington back in the darker days of 1944. The new flag will hang alongside the existing one in the rear right-hand corner of the church.

Pfc. Henry S. Pawlings – New York – KIA June 6th 1944

Pfc. William L. Gray – North Carolina – KIA June 6th 1944

There was a memorial service held for Pfc. Gray at the Belmont Park Methodist Church, Charlotte, North Carolina.

Pvt. Joseph A. Byrne – New York – KIA June 17th 1944

TL Rodgers headstone (Carolina Cemetery in Andalusia, Alabama) was originally incorrectly marked as the 503 Parachute Infantry, it has since been corrected to show the 504.

And finally, for all the fallen from the 504th Parachute Infantry Regiment:

They shall grow not old, as we that are left grow old,
Age shall not weary them, nor the years condemn,
At the going down of the sun, and in the morning,
We will remember them.

Laurence Binyon

When you go home, tell them of us and say:
"For your tomorrow we gave our today."

Appendix A

References and Acknowledgements.

Appendix A – References and Acknowledgements.

In compiling and writing this book I cannot take credit for some of the information it contains. Some of the work is my own, but I have made use of a number of quotes from various peoples memoirs. Some of the information has been drawn from researching a multitude of sources, both in hard copy (books), on the Internet, and from individuals that were involved at the time. I have tried to compile bits of information from a variety of sources to produce a record of the 504 Parachute Infantry Regiment's time at Shady Lane, Evington in Leicestershire.

I have therefore attempted to list below and fully acknowledge with my grateful thanks the sources that I have drawn upon and quoted from during the production of this work.

Copyright Disclaimer.

I have done all I can to trace the owners of the various pieces of material, eg. photographs, cuttings etc. used in this publication. The passage of time has not made the task easy and in some cases impossible. If further information and proof of ownership should be made available then attribution will be given, or if requested the material removed, in any subsequent editions.

Books.

Put on Your Boots and Parachutes
Deryk Wills   By kind permission of Deryk Wills: Deryk Wills (1 Mar 1992)

Brothers in Arms: 'A' Company 504th Parachute Infantry Regiment, 82nd Airborne Division from North Africa to Berlin.
Frank W. van Lunteren   By kind permission of Frank W. van Lunteren: Frank W. van Lunteren (June 2006)

All the Way to Berlin
James Megellas   Presidio Press (March 4, 2003)

Strike and Hold
T. Moffatt Burriss   By kind permission of Potomac Books: Potomac Books (August 2000)

The Devils in Baggy Pants - Combat Record of the 504th PIR, April'43 to July'45
Lt. W.D.Mandle & Pfc. D.H.Whittier

Birds Eye Wartime Leicestershire (1939 – 1945)
Terence C. Cartwright   By kind permission of TCC Publications: TCC Publications (23 Feb 2002)

Those Devils in Baggy Pants
Ross Carter   Buccaneer Books (1951)

Brave Men, Gentle Heroes: American Fathers and Sons in WW2 and Vietnam.
Michael Takiff   William Morrow (October 21, 2003)

Prop Blast – Chronicle of the 504th Parachute Infantry Regiment.
Steven J Mrozek   By kind permission of Steven J Mrozek

All American All the Way
Phil Nordyke   Copyright 2005 © by Phil Nordyke. Reprinted with permission of publisher Zenith Press, an imprint of MBI Publishing Company LLC, St. Paul, MN USA.

Casablanca to VE Day – A Paratrooper's Memoirs'.
Darrell G Harris   By kind permission of Darrell G Harris. (Dorrance Publishing Co. Inc.)

Saga of the All Americans
W. Forrest Dawson   Battery Press (2004)

On to Berlin: Battles of an Airborne Commander, 1943-1946
General James M Gavin   Copyright © 1978 James M Gavin. Used with kind permission of Viking Penguin, a division of Penguin Group (USA) Inc.

Internet Sites.

www.strikehold504th.com

www.eddiesplace.org

www.ww2-airborne.us

www.csupomona.edu/~rosenkrantz/paratroop/sgtdave.htm

www.marketgarden.com

www.clubmobile.org

www.504paratroopers.nl

www.home.hawaii.rr.com/pir504/

www.508pir.org

www.wartimeleicestershire.com

www.bcompany504pir.org

www.freewebs.com/davidstanford504pir/

Authors contact details:
Mr. Peter J. Outridge
17, Fairfield Avenue,
Felixstowe,
Suffolk.
IP11 9JQ
United Kingdom

Email: peteroutridge@yahoo.co.uk